Eastman Curtis has done an excelle[nt] [job...] train our children. His practical, Bib[lical...] get. This book should be requir[ed...] Especially those raising teenagers in today's society.

Joyce Meyer
Bible teacher, Author,
Conference host

If ever a person was hell bent on destruction, devastation, drugs, and disaster, it was Eastman Curtis. It took a miracle to transform his life. But, miraculously, his life was transformed by the saving, healing, delivering power of Jesus Christ. If ever there was a person now heaven bound and speaking with the voice of experience, it is Eastman. The good news is that he is not keeping his heaven-bound experience to himself. It is his burning desire to see that every hell-bent teen becomes heaven-bound. This world needs Eastman's message, and I believe it can bring a transformation in anyone's life.

Richard and Lindsay Roberts
Richard Roberts, President of
Oral Roberts University

Great stuff. Eastman gives us powerful, practical, and Biblical tools to guide our kids. This book works. We see it in scripture; we see it in Eastman's family; and we see it in the Church. Parents, read this book and use it.

Casey Treat
Pastor

RAISING
HEAVEN-BOUND
KIDS IN A
HELL-BENT WORLD

EASTMAN CURTIS

OLIVER
NELSON™

THOMAS NELSON PUBLISHERS
Nashville

Published in Nashville, Tennessee, by Thomas Nelson, Inc.

Scripture quotations noted NKJV are from THE NEW KING JAMES VERSION. Copyright © 1979, 1980, 1982, Thomas Nelson, Inc., Publishers.

Scripture quotations noted NLT are from the *Holy Bible,* New Living Translation, copyright © 1996. Used by permission of Tyndale House Publishers, Inc., Wheaton, Illinois 60189. All rights reserved.

Scripture quotations noted AMPLIFIED are from THE AMPLIFIED BIBLE: Old Testament. Copyright © 1961, 1964 by Zondervan Publishing House (used by permission); and from THE AMPLIFIED NEW TESTAMENT. Copyright © 1958 by the Lockman Foundation (used by permission).

Scripture quotations noted ASV are from the AUTHORIZED VERSION.

Scripture quotations noted TLB are from *The Living Bible,* copyright © 1971. Used by permission of Tyndale House Publishers, Inc., Wheaton, Illinois 60189. All rights reserved.

Scripture quotations noted NIV are from the HOLY BIBLE, NEW INTERNATIONAL VERSION ®. Copyright © 1973, 1978, 1984 by International Bible Society. Used by permission of Zondervan Bible Publishing House. All rights reserved.

The "NIV" and "New International Version" trademarks are registered in the United States Patent and Trademark Office by International Bible Society. Use of either trademark requires the permission of International Bible Society.

Scripture quotations noted KJV are from the Holy Bible, KING JAMES VERSION.

Scripture quotations noted NASB are from the NEW AMERICAN STANDARD BIBLE ®, copyright © 1960, 1962, 1963, 1968, 1971, 1972, 1973, 1975, 1977, The Lockman Foundation. Used by permission. (www.Lockman.org)

Names and details have been changed in order to protect the privacy of individuals and their family members.

Library of Congress Cataloging-in-Publication Data

Curtis, Eastman.
    Raising heaven bound kids in a hell bent world / Eastman Curtis.
        p. cm.
    ISBN 0–7852–6872–3 (pbk.)
    1. Parenting—Religious aspects—Christianity. 2. Teenagers—Religious life. I. Title.

BV4529 .C87 2000
248.8'45—dc21

00–030913
CIP

Printed in the United States of America

1 2 3 4 5 6 — 05 04 03 02 01 00

This book is dedicated to my loving wife, Angel, a true visionary. Back in Bible College when we first met, you saw something in me that no one else could see. Whenever I felt overwhelmed, you believed in me and inspired a heart-felt conviction that I could make it through anything. Your confidence in me and in the call of God on my life has been a constant stream of encouragement. You have proven that if we dare to dream, we can do anything through the power of the Holy Spirit. Your integrity and spirit of excellence have had a marked influence on my life as well as on those around us—continually inspiring me to strive for a better tommorrow. There is no one with whom I would rather share my life than you. I am eternally indebted to God for giving me such a great woman. I have learned that if I meditate on God's Word, pray in faith, and listen to my wife (and not necessarily in that order!), I will make it.

Contents

Acknowledgments

I AM SO GRATEFUL for all the help that went into the writing of this book. This book consists of more than just the knowledge and experiences accumulated during my more than two decades of ministry to teenagers. It is my calling, my passion, to help you with your teenager. The people who helped me with this book took on that same call and passion.

Thank you:

To all the people at Thomas Nelson Publishing for believing in this book and for all the encouragement they have given me.

To Kathleen O'Donnell—your hours of editing and re-editing and re-re-editing have tremendously helped me make (or almost make) my deadlines. This book could not have been accomplished without you.

To Sean Park—your encouragement and dedication to seeing our God-given vision fulfilled have been an inspiration in helping me reach this generation. Thanks for keeping things on track while I've been out of the loop writing this book.

To Mike and Kim Francen, who have been true friends throughout the writing of this book. Your ministry and passion for souls have ignited my heart to bring Jesus to this generation. Thanks for all your input and for letting me bounce hours of ideas off you.

To my children, Sumner and Nicole, who have been so understanding and encouraging while I have been locked in my office working on my book. Thanks for all the fun breaks during the writing of "the book."

Most of all to my wife, Angel, for her patience and truly being the joy of my life. Your unwavering faith in me has encouraged me to go beyond my own abilities.

Foreword

GET READY for a special blessing on your life! By picking up this book, you are telling God that you want to be a better parent. He sees your desire to help your teens experience the best life that they possibly can, to help them know God and walk according to His precepts. God singled out Abraham from all the other people on earth and chose to make His covenant with him because He knew that Abraham would pass it on to his children:

> *I have known him, in order that he may command his children and his household after him, that they keep the way of the LORD, to do righteousness and justice, that the LORD may bring to Abraham what He has spoken to him.* (Gen. 18:19 NKJV)

When God sees you instructing your children, He takes great delight in you and qualifies you as a candidate to receive His many enormous benefits. Remember that you are not in this alone, even if you are a single parent. God is helping you, rolling up His sleeves and getting involved with your teenagers.

You may feel that you have made too many mistakes in the past, but remember that everyone else has made mistakes too. There is only one perfect parent, and that is our heavenly Father. And there is only one perfect child: Jesus. Even if you have made a mess of parenting, it is never too late to start over. God has promised you that He will give you back what you lost to the "stripping locusts, the cutting locusts, the swarming locusts, and the hopping locusts" (Joel 2:25 NLT). This is your time for restoration, your time to take back all that the enemy has tried to steal from you. This is the beginning of your breakthrough.

What an exciting time to be alive! Many people don't look at it this way; they love to focus on the negative. They focus on the increase in crime and immorality. They point to the fact that sexually transmitted diseases have reached epidemic proportions. They note that, with stories of road rage and school shootings continually broadcasting on the news, random acts of violence have become a way of life for many. But there is good news: "Where sin abounded, grace abounded much more" (Rom. 5:20 NKJV). Another translation puts it this way: "As people sinned more and more, God's wonderful kindness became more abundant" (NLT). With the outbreak of sin, God is moving in with much more grace.

God has made a way for us to live in a hell-bent world and still have a bit of heaven on earth. Jesus instructed us to pray: "Your kingdom come. / Your will be done / On earth as it is in heaven" (Matt. 6:10 NKJV). This book is designed to help you experience God's kingdom and His will here on earth with your family. Get ready for the most challenging but rewarding part of parenting: raising heaven-bound kids in a hell-bent world!

1

The Power of Positive Words

WE'VE ALL heard the nursery rhyme that says: "Sticks and stones may break my bones, but words will never hurt me." The truth is, words can hurt—especially the words we speak over our children.

While speaking to the disciples on the subject of faith, Jesus provided us with a powerful illustration of this truth: "Whoever says to this mountain, 'Be removed and be cast into the sea,' and does not doubt in his heart, but believes that those things he says will be done, he will have whatever he says" (Mark 11:23 NKJV). Through this teaching, Jesus plainly tells us we can have what we believe in when our words are mixed with faith from the heart. We must understand that faith can be either positive or negative in nature. Negative faith is simply another term for *fear*. Eventually we will come to believe what we say. And what we believe will materialize in our lives. Jesus taught that we can have what we ask for, whether good or bad. If we train our hearts to meditate on the positive promises contained in the Word and tutor our mouths to declare those promises, it will produce powerful results in our lives.

Two exasperated parents recently approached me with their son. The father said, "I need your help with my teenager!" He then proceeded to tell me that his teen would never amount to anything, describing him as a very rebellious person. The mother stood there nodding her head in agreement. I watched as that young man began to close up and emotionally drift farther away from his irritated parents. In fact, I could practically see an invisible barrier go up. The sad thing was that Mom and Dad were not even aware of the barrier they were putting up between themselves and their son.

When the dad finished blasting him, I turned and looked at the boy. This young man was so embarrassed that he was unable even to look at me. Undaunted, I extended my hand to him and said, "Mom and Dad, I can spot a winner, and this young man is going to be a winner!" You would not believe the transformation that took place right before my eyes. Gazing up at me, the young man broke into a big grin and shook my hand like a person who was going to change the world. Now he was hanging on to words of life rather than death!

When I spoke with his parents privately, they were astonished at how their son had warmed up to me. The reason he liked me? I chose to believe the best in that young man, just as God has chosen to believe the best in me. Sometimes it is easier to see the best in people when we are not so close to them. The funny thing is, the most important people in our lives are those closest to us. It's imperative to declare the promises of God unashamedly over our friends, our families, and especially over our children.

"Death and life are in the power of the tongue, / And those who love it will eat its fruit" (Prov. 18:21 NKJV). What kind of fruit are you eating? Make it a point to talk your teenager "up" and not "down." The way you talk about and to your teen greatly determines what he will actually become. Our words charge the atmosphere around our children with either life or death, success or failure. Choose to let your words be a fountain of life. You may not see results today, but keep at it. Change is coming. You can be confident that God will complete the work He began in your teen's life. You have His Word on it.

protect your children if offered up by a heart filled with fear and anxiety. Jesus taught us that "whatever things you ask for in prayer, believing, you will receive" (Matt. 21:22 NKJV). Remember, it is not just prayer, but believing prayer, that changes things.

Stop! Take control of your thoughts concerning your son or daughter right now. Yes, pray! And pray often. But don't let fear control your thought life. One of the greatest discoveries I have made is that I do not have to be controlled by my thoughts. Rather, I have the power to control my thought life. The word *worry* is actually derived from an old Anglo-Saxon term meaning "to strangle" or "to choke." Worry chokes the life out of the very faith that seeks to surround and protect your child:

> Modern medical research has proven that worry breaks down resistance to disease. More than that, it actually diseases the nervous system—particularly that of the digestive organs and of the heart. Add to this the toll in unhappiness of sleepless nights and void of internal sunshine, and you have a glimpse of the work this monster does in destroying the effectiveness of the human body.[1]

If worry can do that to the human body, then what power does it have over your relationship with your child? Taking control of fearful thoughts concerning your children is the first step to releasing the power of God on their behalf. We can literally turn our fear into faith by focusing our thoughts on the promises contained in the Word of God rather than on the fears of the world. Whatever you think about your children will become your expectation of them.

Affirmation: *I choose to live in faith concerning my child. I take every evil thought captive, and I cast down every worry and thought of fear! I purpose to see _____(child's name) through the eyes of* *faith. I thank You that You surround her with Your mighty angels. I believe she will not walk to the right or the left, but on straight paths of righteousness.*

Affirmation Scriptures:

Hebrews 11:6; 2 Corinthians 10:5; Psalm 91:11; Proverbs 4:27; and Psalm 23:3.

3

Control Your Thinking

ONE OF THE GREATEST revelations we can have as Christians is to understand that we can control our thought life rather than allow our thought life to control us. We can also put this ability to work in our role as parents and use it to help us train up our children in the right way. We can use it to magnify the good in them rather than focusing on what is bad.

In 2 Corinthians 10:4–5 we are told,

> For the weapons of our warfare are not carnal but mighty in God for pulling down strongholds, casting down arguments and every high thing that exalts itself against the knowledge of God, bringing every thought into captivity to the obedience of Christ. (NKJV)

The key here is that we have the ability to bring into captivity every thought to obedience to Christ. It is not something beyond our reach. It just requires some action on our part.

Remember that the enemy will always try to magnify himself (Lam. 1:9). That word *magnify* means "to enlarge in fact or in appearance," "to exaggerate."[1] Think of how the enemy always seems to stick the worst thoughts in your mind about your child. Given the opportunity, the devil will try to turn a headache into a brain tumor in your mind. If you have a pain in your chest, the devil will tell you that it is a heart attack when it is actually just indigestion. God specifically tells us that we are supposed to keep our thoughts (including our thoughts about our kids) focused on good things:

> Finally, brethren, whatever things are true, whatever things are noble, whatever things are just, whatever things are pure, whatever things are lovely, whatever things are of good report, if there is any virtue and if there is anything praiseworthy—meditate on these things. (Phil. 4:8 NKJV)

This is where I believe many parents have gone wrong. Failing to acknowledge the things their child does right, they always tell him what he has done wrong instead. They magnify the bad rather than the good. This is harmful. We are to meditate on the good report concerning our children and not on negative imaginations. The things we think about them are the things that will magnify in their lives. This is what Philippians 4:8 is all about: magnifying the positive and not the negative. We need to keep our thoughts focused on the things that are true, honest, just, noble, and of good report. Make the good report about your child your focus.

Affirmation: *I choose to magnify the good things in my teen and not the bad. I am quick to listen, slow to speak, and slow to become angry. Thank You that only good and edifying words about him come forth from my mouth. I bring every thought concerning my child into obedience to Christ and focus on those that are of good report.*

Affirmation Scriptures:
2 Corinthians 10:5; Philippians 4:8; James 1:19;
and Proverbs 21:23.

4

You Are What You Think

YOU ARE WHAT you think. Be careful about the things on which you meditate because they are what you will become. In Proverbs 23:7 we are told that as a man thinks in his heart, so is he. Not only will your thought life affect you, but it will also affect your teenager. It can impact her behavior for good or for evil. It can even help change the course of her destiny.

My dad's view of me when I was a kid had a tremendous impact on me, even after I was saved and set free from drugs and alcohol. He had created a mental picture of me as a loser and a failure. Because he saw me as a loser and a failure, I acted like one whenever I was around him. I said and did the dumbest things. One day I began to realize that the reason I acted that way around him was because that was the way he saw me. I had conformed my own behavior to mirror his perception of me. I literally had to change the manner in which I perceived myself when I was with my father. Once I began to change my own mental image of myself, it was easy for me to change my behavior as well. It's a whole lot easier for teenagers to effect change in their lives if their parents can also envision them as changed for the better.

As we have already seen, the Word plainly tells us that as a man thinks in his heart, so is he. A good illustration of this truth can be found in Numbers 13:33. The children of Israel were about to enter into the promised land and had commissioned spies to scope out the land. Many of those sent out reported that they saw giants (Anak's descendants, a people who were "great and tall"). Not only were these spies like grasshoppers in their own sight, but they were also grasshoppers in the sight of the inhabitants of the land. The way they saw themselves was identical to the way in which others perceived them. Because they refused to view themselves the way God saw them—fully capable of defeating all opposition—they ended up wandering around in the wilderness for forty years instead of reaching the promised land right away. They were defeated by their own negative perceptions.

To be effective, you must see yourself as a good parent. You may not have all the right answers, but you do have *the* Answer—Jesus Christ. God is going to help you through this thing. You're going to train up a child who is a winner and not a loser. This comes back to our original premise that you are what you think and that is what you will become. Start thinking of yourself as an effective parent and of your teenager as a godly, successful person. Then watch in amazement as you begin to see the transformation that will take place in both your lives!

Affirmation: *I thank You, Lord, that I am an effective parent. I am training up a winner and not a loser. Everything _____ (child's name) puts her hands to prospers because her soul is prospering. I bring all my thoughts concerning my child and myself as a parent into submission to God's Word. I think only on the things that are of good report, those things that are honorable and uplifting.*

Affirmation Scriptures:
Philippians 4:8; 2 Corinthians 10:5; and 3 John 3.

5

Self-Image, Self-Talk

YOUR SELF-IMAGE is directly linked to the words you speak about yourself. Many times we do not realize how powerful our words are. In fact, our words are containers, either for death or for life: "Death and life are in the power of the tongue" (Prov. 18:21 NKJV). Ecclesiastes 10:12 tells us that "the words of a wise man's mouth are gracious, / But the lips of a fool shall swallow him up." Often we get swallowed up by low self-esteem and feelings of inadequacy when it comes to the challenge of raising our children. This happens because of the negative words we speak about ourselves. Words like "I'm so confused. I don't know what I'm going to do with my child. I'm not a good parent." Or "I don't understand what they are going through." The more you begin to talk like that, the more you will reinforce your sense of inadequacy.

Ephesians 5:19 says that we need to speak to one another in psalms and hymns and spiritual songs, singing and making melody in our hearts to the Lord. We also need to speak to ourselves in this way. Once when I was seeking God's direction to help me make a decision, I began saying, "I don't know what I'm going to do. I am so confused. I'm not hearing the voice of God. I don't know the next step I need to take." The more I said these negative things about myself, the more confused I became. But then I began to declare, "I know the voice of my Father. I have a right to be led by the Spirit because I am a child of God." I began to quote Scripture and make the following affirmation:

11

"I hear my Father's voice. The voice of a stranger, I do not know. God is leading me. God is showing me." All of a sudden, God's direction became clear to me. Understanding God's direction was a direct result of the faith-filled words I had begun to speak.

This same principle applies to God's direction in raising your child. You can lean on God, and He will give you wisdom. He will give you revelation and understanding on how to train up your child or teenager in the way he should go. But you must speak words of confidence, words that recognize His help, and words of faith in His ability to effectively communicate His wisdom to you.

Affirmation: *Thank You, Lord, that I am filled with wisdom and understanding as a parent. My mouth utters wisdom and my tongue speaks what is just. I speak only faith-filled words, words that recognize Your ability to communicate with me and show me how to raise my child. I find my self-worth in You and know that I can do all things through the strength that Christ gives me.*

Affirmation Scriptures:
Psalm 37:30; Psalm 19:14; Philippians 4:13; and Proverbs 21:23.

6

I Am the Boss (Or "Take Control Early")

HOPEFULLY, you're reading this book before your child actually becomes a teenager. But often people wait for a crisis situation before they act. Then they run out and buy as much stuff on the subject area as they possibly can, hoping to make right those areas that are wrong. Well, no matter how late in the game it is or at what stage your teenager or you are, it's not too late to intervene. God is able to restore all the years that have gotten messed up, because He is a God of restoration.

Ephesians 6:1 says, "Children, obey your parents in the Lord, for this is right." Then it goes on to say "'Honor your father and mother,' which is the first commandment with promise: 'that it may be well with you and you may live long on the earth'" (vv. 2–3 NKJV). Obedience on the part of your teen is important, but so is her attitude. That is why the Word commands us not only to obey our parents, but also to honor them. I like to use the following illustration to show the difference between simply obeying and obeying with honor: When you ask your child to take out the trash, she rolls her eyes, gets mad, and throws stuff around. Grabbing up the trash, she ends up throwing it outside. She is being obedient, but she is not showing honor. When you honor somebody, not only do you do as he has requested, but you also do it willingly and with a good heart. If people want to live long and experience abundant life, they must have a good attitude.

As the boss of our children, we are not to provoke them to anger.

However, we are to be concerned with their attitude. When you see a bad attitude beginning to rise up in your teen, sit down and talk with her about it. You need to let her know that you have noticed some attitudes that are not right. Tell her that you want to sit down and talk with her because you want what is best for her. If your teenager sees that you really are concerned, she may "buck in the chute" at first, but in the long haul, love will always prevail. Being the boss does not mean you have to jump up and down or scream and yell. It means that you are confident of your authority and you don't have to prove it. You know who you are.

What would you think if a policeman pulled you over, ran over to you, and started jumping up and down and yelling, "Why were you speeding? You know you're not supposed to speed"? Ranting and raving, he then got mad and threw his clipboard down. Well, I am confident that most of us would lose a lot of respect for him. But, if that same police officer, instead of losing his temper, calmly explained the situation to you, he would be much more likely to earn your respect. Being the boss does not mean you are free to go berserk with your emotions. Rather, it means you are a strong, solid, loving, and kind leader.

Affirmation: *I thank You, Lord, that my child obeys me with a willing heart. I lovingly and firmly lead her in the right path and do not provoke her to anger. Because she seeks to honor her father and mother, she experiences abundant life to its fullest.*

Affirmation Scriptures:
Deuteronomy 28:2–8; Proverbs 22:6; Ephesians 6:1–4; and 1 Peter 5:3–5.

7

Setting Up House Rules and Standards

ONE OF THE MOST important things you can do as a parent is to set up house rules and standards for your teen. Establishing boundaries for your teenager will cause him to take responsibility for his own actions. This may surprise a lot of people, but setting up rules and standards will breed security because it will provide your child with clear boundaries. In reality, teenagers desire these clearly defined parameters. They may not realize they want limits, but I can tell you this: They really do need rules. From working with teenagers over the last eighteen years, I'm convinced they need established boundaries beyond which they are not allowed to go. Once they receive established limits, they can chart a corresponding course for their behavior.

In Psalm 106:43–44 we are told: "Many times He delivered them; / But they rebelled in their counsel, / And were brought low for their iniquity. / Nevertheless He regarded their affliction, / when He heard their cry" (NKJV). Here we see people who lived under the blessings of God when they were obedient to the Word and to the borders and parameters that God had set up for their lives. But these same people invariably rebelled and strayed from the rules and the principles God had set up for them. As a result of their disobedience, they were brought low, and the enemy came in and clobbered them. Every time, even in the midst of their goof-ups and messes, they cried out to their God for mercy. And the amazing thing is, God had mercy on them and delivered them.

However, they still suffered certain consequences for their actions. We have to be taught responsibility for our actions. Teaching our kids rules and regulations along with the consequences that come from breaching those standards will help them learn to be responsible.

Years ago, when I was a youth pastor, I knew a young man who was continually goofing off and exerting a bad influence on a number of the teenagers in our youth group. He was one of the deacons' sons. Finally, after many months of working with this guy, I told him I was going to have to kick him out of the youth group. He would not be able to come to youth group anymore because of his negative influence on the other kids. I told him I loved him, but that I was going to have to stop him from attending the youth meetings if he did not change.

Well, sure enough, he goofed off the next week and did the same thing as before. So I kicked him out of youth group. His parents came in and talked to me about their "little angel" and how he could never do anything like that. I explained to them that this had been building up for quite a while and that I had talked to him about taking responsibility for his actions. I let them know that if he wanted to come back into the youth group, I would have to set up certain parameters for him as part of a discipleship program.

Because he did not want to abide by my requirements, he left the youth group. But about three months later at around two in the morning, I got a telephone call from the county jail. The young man had been arrested for vandalism; he had been doing some destructive things. The guy had just one phone call, and he made it to me. It amazed me that he called me rather than his mom and dad, who let him get away with everything. He called me because he knew I loved him and would set up rules and parameters for him. Confident that I cared about him, he also knew I would help him. I picked him up and discipled him back into faith. Now he's serving God, has a family, and is doing great.

Teenagers scream for borders. They scream for people to give them some parameters for their lives. True, once a boundary is put into place, they will run up and stick their toe right up to it. But they must understand that consequences exist for breaking those rules and regulations. Understanding those consequences will benefit them for the rest of their lives.

As our children grow up, though, we need to loosen our grip on them. When they were young, we set tons of rules and regulations for them to obey. We didn't even let them go out into the front yard alone. Letting go can sometimes be very difficult. We want to protect our children from making wrong decisions and getting hurt. But if we teach our children how to act based on principle and not just according to rules, we will help them learn to make good decisions for the rest of their lives. It will help them understand that with maturity comes responsibility. Then we will be able to let go with confidence, knowing that they are capable of making wise and godly decisions on their own.

Affirmation: *I thank You, Lord, that _____ (name of child) walks in godly obedience, obeying Your plan because of his faith. He understands that when he chooses to obey the rules of our home, he is bringing the blessings of obedience upon himself. He honors us as his parents, esteeming and valuing as precious those in authority over him, ensuring that all will go well with him and his future.*

Affirmation Scriptures:
Romans 1:5; Deuteronomy 28:8; and Ephesians 6:1–3.

8

It Is Never Too Late:
Restoring the Years of the Cankerworm

MANY PARENTS tell me that they have let things slide with their teenagers for so long that they have lost all hope of changing them. These parents believe their teens are set in their ways and immovable. But the good news is that there is hope, no matter where you are in your relationship with your child. If you will begin applying biblical principles, you will see results. Joel 2:25 says: "And I will restore to you the years that the locust hath eaten, the canker-worm and the caterpillar, and the palmer-worm, my great army which I sent among you" (ASV). God is a God of restoration. Even if years have gone by, God is able to restore those lost years with your teenager.

Some parents came to me a while back about their son and told me they had only recently become Christians. They knew they hadn't trained up their child the right way. In fact, they used to go out drinking and partying with their teenager. So they asked me what they could do now to improve their relationship with him. I told them that God is a God of restoration—that He is able to restore the years they had messed up. We sat down right there and talked about the situation with their teen. I encouraged them to sit down with their teenager and explain to him that they realized they had not been the best parents they could have been, but that they wanted to work on their relationship.

This couple could not wait to begin working on the situation—they believed God would restore all the years they had messed up. And He did. The young man completely turned his life around because his parents took the time to sit down and communicate their hearts to him. They let him know the direction they wanted to head, that all they wanted was the best for him. That young man got saved and is now serving God. No matter how badly you may have messed up in the past, it is not too late to start now. God is still a God of restoration.

Affirmation: *I choose to forget the mistakes of the past. God is doing a new thing in my relationship with my child. He is making a way for us; He is restoring those years of failure and disappointment. God is still a God of restoration, and He is continually working in my relationship with my child.*

Affirmation Scriptures:
Philippians 3:13–14; Isaiah 43:18–19; and Joel 2:25.

9

Starting Somewhere

WHEN WE TALK about training up our children and raising heaven-bound kids in a hell-bent world, the first thing we must realize is that change has to begin with us. It must begin with us and not with our child. Once our attitudes change, our children's attitudes will also change.

God wants us to have success in training up our children, but the only way we can succeed is if we are doers of the Word. In Joshua 1:8 we are commanded,

> This Book of the Law shall not depart from your mouth, but you shall meditate in it day and night, that you may observe to do according to all that is written in it. For then you will make your way prosperous, and then you will have good success. (NKJV)

This Scripture lays out the whole reason why we confess the Word and keep it from departing from our mouths, why we meditate on the Word day and night so that we might do all that is written. Once we do these things, our ways will be made prosperous, and we will have success. Although prayer and the study of these principles are very important (as is releasing our faith for our children), we need to implement these principles in our lives. We must take action. Knowing I need to spend time with my teenager in order to influence him will not accomplish anything unless I actually set aside the time to do it. It's not

20

just knowing the right thing to do that counts; it is *doing* it. What you do with what you know will make the difference. First John 3:18 lays this out plainly: "My little children, let us not love in word or in tongue, but in deed and in truth" (NKJV).

So don't just tell other people you love your children; make sure you tell *your children*. When you see them doing something right, compliment them. If you see them doing a great job, tell them they did a great job. And remember, just knowing you should do these things is not enough. You must actually do them.

Affirmation: *I am continually being conformed to the image of God both in my words and actions. God is working in me, causing me to desire to do His will and helping me to see my child as God sees him. My attitude toward my child is filled with faith and hope, and he lovingly responds to the changes that God is effecting in my heart.*

Affirmation Scriptures:
Philippians 1:6; Philippians 2:13; and 1 John 3:18.

10

Time: Quantity and Quality

IT SEEMS AS THOUGH everything in today's society screams for our time and attention—our jobs, recreational habits, churches, and families. But the challenge is that we have only twenty-four hours in each day to accomplish everything. So we begin to justify our thinking and say to ourselves, "Well, I'm not really able to spend a lot of time with my children. They're busy doing their own thing anyway, and I'm busy doing mine." We rationalize that the time we actually spend with them is quality time even though it is not quantity time.

But we've got to blast through that sort of idea, because in reality, quality time *is* quantity time. The key thing we need to do is to prioritize our time according to the things that matter most. If you love someone or something, you are going to spend time with that person or thing. And teenagers are the first to recognize the reality of that fact. You can tell them you love them all you want, but unless you actually spend time with them, they'll know differently.

Some time ago, I met a youth pastor in the north-central United States. This person had one of the largest youth groups in that region. The interesting thing about it was that this lady didn't wear "hip" clothes or use "hip" language. In fact, she looked like Momma Cass of the Mamas and the Papas, and everyone affectionately referred to her as "Momma Cass wearing tie-dyed muumuus."

Wondering how she came to have such a large youth group, I began to talk to her teenagers. Here is what some of them told me. Whenever they played basketball, this youth pastor showed up even though their own parents didn't come. Every time they made a basket or completed a great play, they looked up into the stands and saw her watching them and cheering for them. Spending quantity time as well as quality time with these teenagers was the secret behind her success as a youth pastor and behind her ability to build strong relationships with her youth group.

If you want to be successful as a parent, you are going to have to spend quantity time as well as quality time with your children. Trying to carve out a small bit of quality time during the week just won't cut it. Spending real time with your child lets her know that you love her and enjoy being with her. So make it your aim to spend more time with your teen. Let her know she is your priority.

Affirmation: *I make it my aim to spend quantity, as well as quality, time with my child. Because I have made her my priority, she is solidly convinced that I love her and seek her best. She is confident of my love and support, helping her to successfully meet life's challenges without fear or insecurity.*

Affirmation Scriptures:
John 13:34–35; 1 John 3:18; and Luke 1:17.

11

Get Rid of the Guilt When Abel Turns into Cain

THE ONE THING you have to remember as a parent is that your child has his own free will. Poor behavior on his part isn't always a direct reflection of the way you have trained him or of the way you have brought him up. He has made his own choices in life as well.

The effects of a child's own choices in his life are exemplified in the story of Cain and Abel in Genesis 4. Although both boys came from the same parents, the one was great and the other, well, was not so good. Brought up in the same family, they still turned out completely different. And in parenting we have to remember that perfect parents do not exist. In fact, there is only one perfect parent, and that is our heavenly Father.

In the midst of everything, there will be times when we mess up. But we can deal with the guilt, and we can right the wrongs we have done. We have not obtained perfection yet, but we are always striving for it. We forget those things that lie behind and we press on to the things that lie ahead.

Guilt and condemnation are two of the greatest things that will keep us from effective parenting, effective relationships with our spouses, effective business dealings, and effective relationships with God. In fact, if the enemy can hold you in an arena of condemnation, he can prevent you from operating in faith. That is why, I believe, the apostle Paul was so adamant about remaining free from guilt. In Romans 8:1 he declared: "There is therefore now no condemnation to those who are in Christ Jesus, who do not walk according to the flesh, but according to the Spirit" (NKJV). God wants us to be free from guilt—free from feelings of inferiority and insecurity. He wants us to realize that through Jesus Christ we can be free from condemnation.

If we do mess up in a particular area of our lives, we need to do two things. The first one is to repent—to take responsibility for our actions. Whether we have disciplined a child too severely or had a wrong attitude about something, we have done wrong.

Next, we need to confess our sin, not try to cover it up or make an excuse for it. We can't blame our wrongdoing on our child's behavior—we have to take responsibility for our own actions. When our teenagers see us accept responsibility for what we have done, they will learn from our example. But if they see us shifting blame, that is exactly what they will learn to do. I believe there is nothing so important as taking responsibility for our own actions. First John 1:9 says, "if we confess our sins, He is faithful and just to forgive us our sins and to cleanse us from all unrighteousness" (NKJV). This Scripture plainly lays out our course of action: The first thing we do is repent of our sin. Then we need to approach the person we wronged and ask that person to forgive us.

God is very concerned about our relationships with other people, especially those with our family. Matthew 5:23–24 says, "Therefore if you bring your gift to the altar, and there remember that your brother has something against you, leave your gift there before the altar, and go your way. First be reconciled to your brother, and then come and offer your gift" (NKJV).

From this Scripture we can see that God wants us to make it right with those we have hurt. Once we repent and ask them for forgiveness, the Bible tells us that God will cleanse our "conscience from dead works to serve the living God" (Heb. 9:14 NKJV). That's the good news. You don't have to stay bound up with guilt or condemnation. The just man may fall seven times, but he will always get back up again.

Affirmation: *I am quick to repent when I do wrong and quick to forgive those who hurt me. Guilt has no hold over me because I know that the blood of Jesus cleanses me from all sin. I recognize that my child exercises his free will and is responsible for his own choices. I thank You, Lord, that my child is also quick to repent when he makes wrong choices and able to turn to You, confident of Your forgiveness.*

Affirmation Scriptures:

1 John 1:9; Matthew 6:14; James 5:16; Hebrews 4:16; Hebrews 9:14; and Ephesians 4:32.

12

Consistency in Discipline

WHEN IT COMES to discipline, consistency is one of the most important factors in success. One thing I have heard over and over again in talking to teenagers from across the nation is "I don't know what my parents want from me." The primary reason for their confusion is that many times parents are not consistent in their discipline.

Let us take the example of a teenager who comes in late after a date or after going out somewhere at night. Sometimes the parent simply looks up from his or her chair and says, "Good to have you home." But the following week, that same parent flips out when the teenager comes home late—even though the teen is not as late as she was the week before. This time the parent's face starts to flush as his anger rises until, finally, harsh words come spewing out of his mouth. Conflicting reactions such as this fail to give a consistent message. Not only is this extremely confusing to teens, but it will also breed instability in them.

We've got to major on the majors and minor on the minors—and be consistent about it. When Jesus talked about the Sadducees and the Pharisees in Matthew 23:24, He called them "blind guides, who strain out a gnat and swallow a camel!" (NKJV). So many times we are the same when it comes to the area of discipline. We end up blowing our stack over minor things and letting major acts of disobedience just slide by.

The good thing about God is that He is always consistent. When it comes to His love for us, it is not based on emotions or dependent on whether He's having a good day or a bad day. God is always having a great day because He is the One who made the day. Hebrews 13:8 says, "Jesus Christ is the same yesterday, today, and forever" (NKJV). If we want to be like our heavenly Father, we cannot allow the personal things we are going through to affect the way we discipline our teenager or how we respond to what she does. We must be consistent in our discipline. That consistency will breed security, and security will breed confidence.

Affirmation: *I thank You, Lord, that I am raising our teen in Your nurture and admonition. Majoring on what is important, I am consistent in my discipline. My teen is secure and confident in knowing where her parents stand on the issues.*

Affirmation Scriptures:
Proverbs 6:23; Proverbs 22:6; and Ephesians 6:4.

13

Discipline Without
Relationship Breeds Rebellion

IN MY DEALINGS with thousands of teenagers each year, the number-one desire I have heard expressed by them is to have a great relationship with Mom and Dad. They may not always show it, and at times they really do not even know how to show it. The sad thing is that most adults are waiting for their teen to take the first step in bridging that relationship. But the responsibility actually rests on the parents' shoulders. Now think about this: Why would a teenager say he just can't seem to live up to his parents' expectations unless the only time his parents talk to him is to correct him? That is why building a relationship with your teenager is so important. Building a relationship includes coming alongside your teen and encouraging him when you see him doing something right, not just correcting him when you see him doing something wrong.

Hebrews says, "If God doesn't discipline you as he does all of his children, it means that you are illegitimate and are not really his children after all" (12:8 NLT). The word *child* here means "one follower of another." It does not mean someone who is being pushed or manipulated by another person, but rather one who is being led. This speaks of relationship and not just discipline.

It is extremely important for you to have fun with your teenager. As a parent, you need to be downright determined that you are going to enjoy your child. Spend time with your teen. Do things together.

It may take work for you to accomplish this, but remember that change has to start with you first. Change has to take place in your heart before it is ever going to happen in your teenager's heart. If all you do is to continually correct and discipline him, it will only serve to provoke him to rebellion. But if you discipline and correct him from the foundation of a solid relationship, it will produce character and a change in heart.

Affirmation: *Heavenly Father, I praise You for showing me how to raise my child according to Your training and instruction. Thank You for a healthy relationship with him, one that is based on mutual love and respect. Secure in the knowledge that he is deeply loved and cared for, he is quick to respond to instruction and seeks to please God and his parents.*

Affirmation Scriptures:
Ephesians 6:4; 1 Corinthians 13:8; and Colossians 3:21.

14

Love Means Discipline

IN TODAY'S WORLD, the word *discipline* is often viewed as a dirty word. Because the world's system always stands in contradiction to the Word of God, many have bought into the lie that a loving parent will not discipline his or her child. Discipline is seen as harsh and void of mercy or compassion. But the truth is, if we love our children, we'll discipline them.

The Bible tells us that one of the ways we love our children is by disciplining them: "If you refuse to discipline your children, it proves you don't love them; if you love your children, you will be prompt to discipline them" (Prov. 13:24 NLT). Since the beginning of creation, God has placed parents in the lives of children to train them up properly and prevent them from going astray later.

But today's society says you need to leave your child alone to let her develop and grow up right. That concept stands completely contrary to the Word of God. Proverbs 29:15 says, "A child left to himself brings shame to his mother" (NKJV). We can take that statement one step further and say that a child left to herself will bring shame to her entire family. God has placed you in your child's life for you to speak words of direction and encouragement to her, for you to influence her in ways that no one else can. Don't buy into the world's lie that you're meant to be a buddy to your child. God has placed you in your child's life to provide her with instruction and correction.

When I was growing up, my dad occasionally used to take me

out to dinner alone with him. That time spent together, just the two of us, meant more to me than any other thing he did for me. It told me I was valuable enough to him that he would take time out just to spend with me. Those outings together significantly impacted me while I was growing up, both as a young child and later on as a teenager.

King David really messed up the training of his children by failing to discipline them. This caused problems later on, as exemplified by the actions of his son Adonijah. First Kings 1:6 tells us, "His father, King David, had never disciplined him at any time, even by asking, 'What you are doing?'" (NLT). As a result of David's failure to discipline his son, Adonijah illegally tried to take over the kingdom (which rightfully belonged to Solomon). When his attempted takeover failed, Adonijah begged for mercy. Solomon gave in the first time, but when he attempted to do it again after David's death, Solomon had Adonijah put to death.

The whole reason Adonijah rebelled was because King David had never disciplined him, not even once. Because David failed in his parental duty to discipline Adonijah, we might say that David shared responsibility for Adonijah's rebellion and subsequent downfall.

Many parents ask me whether it is still possible after their child reaches adolescence to make up for a lack of discipline during the early years. The answer to that question is yes. It may be a little more difficult than doing it right the first time, but you can still accomplish it because of the restorative nature of God. The good thing about God is that He completes any work He begins in us, even in the area of parenting. So it's not too late to start—no matter where you are with your child.

One story of God's restorative power that particularly impresses me is that of a pastor with eight children. One year, during the Thanksgiving holiday, one of his little girls wrapped her arms around him and said, "Dad, I always feel like you're putting the ministry before your children." There was a lot of truth to that statement, the pastor said. Even though half of his kids were already grown, he realized it was not too late to start. That was a real turning point in his life. The pastor set his hand to getting his priorities right with his kids. He knew he had succeeded when one of his grown sons wrote him to tell him how God had restored their relationship.

The success of a parent trying to undo the damage caused by an earlier failure to love and discipline greatly depends not only upon the child's openness but also upon the parent's heart. Children find great security in knowing their parents are concerned about their welfare and destiny. If a teenager understands that Mom and Dad are looking out for her best interests, she'll be a lot more likely to put up with her parent's failures.

When introducing discipline into a teenager's life for the first time, you must acknowledge your earlier failure to discipline and love your child properly. Being honest with your child will break down many of the barriers standing between you. Admitting your shortcomings may be difficult—we all have a strong tendency to cover up our mistakes. But as you confess your mistakes to your child and agree to work on changing them, your child will realize that you are making an honest effort to open up the communication lines between parent and teenager.

Next, you need to ask your child to share her deepest need with you. Because teenagers are not always willing to communicate with their parents, you may have to look for an opportunity to discover that need. Regardless of whether you know the details of her need, you can still help her. Desperate desire for a parent's love and help exists in every teen's life. Remember, love means discipline. If you love your children, you will be prompt to discipline them (Prov. 13:24).

Affirmation: *Heavenly Father, I praise You for showing me how to bring up my child with training and instruction from You. You are restoring our* *relationship and making up for any failure on my part to discipline or love her correctly when she was young. Thank You for sending Your Word to help her find her divine destiny and walk a self-disciplined life.*

Affirmation Scriptures:

Ephesians 6:4; Proverbs 1:3; Proverbs 6:23; and John 10:10.

15

Self-Control

ALBERT SCHWEITZER, a distinguished musician, theologian, and medical missionary at the turn of the century, once said, "Example is not the main thing influencing others, it is the only thing."[1] If we desire to see our children exercise self-control, we must first develop it ourselves. We need to work on self-control the same way we work on any fruit of the Spirit. First, we must recognize the importance of self-control. Next, we need to set our hand to developing discipline in all areas of our lives. When your teenager sees you respond to tough situations without losing control, you will effectively preach volumes to him, much more than can be accomplished through hours of personal lectures.

A father once told me about his own experience with helping his son develop self-control. Noticing that his son lacked this particular fruit of the Spirit, he decided to confront him about it. Before he had a chance to do so, however, he felt the Spirit of the Lord begin to deal with him. He realized that his son lacked self-control because he lacked it too.

After seeking the Lord for direction, he recognized he needed to develop discipline in certain areas of his own life. The father then decided to apologize to his son for failing to set a good example. Next, he began to incorporate discipline into his everyday life through consistent Bible reading, prayer, and personal devotions. The change in his father had such influence on the boy that shortly afterward, the son also began to change. The difference in his son was so dramatic that the boy's baseball coach called the father to ask what he had done to effect such improvement. The boy's attitude had changed, and he no longer had a temper. The father responded, "My son has changed because I have changed."

Watching you react to difficult situations with self-control and restraint will breed stability and confidence in your teen. That is how change starts. We are able to help our children develop self-discipline because we have learned how to do it ourselves. Romans 5:3 says, "We can rejoice, too, when we run into problems and trials, for we know that they are good for us—they help us learn to endure" (NLT).

Affirmation: *Father, I thank You that I walk in the fruit of the Spirit in every area of my life. Because I exercise self-control, I am able to effectively teach _____ (child's name) how to develop self-control. _____ (child's name) lives a disciplined lifestyle, producing confidence and stability in his relationship with God and in his God-given destiny.*

Affirmation Scriptures:
Ephesians 6:4; Proverbs 6:23; and Galatians 5:22.

16

Parenting Requires Teamwork

RESEARCH HAS SHOWN that the most stable environment for a teenager is in a family having both a mother and a father.[1] Within the family unit, it is essential that both parents work together in training up their children.

Now, if you are reading this and are a single parent, please don't throw in the towel. You can still raise up great kids. I'm convinced that God will give you supernatural grace to train your children right, especially during their teenage years. Although the most stable situation is in a home with both a mom and a dad, God is still able to work in single-parent families.

I believe there are four important keys to raising up heaven-bound children in a hell-bent world. The first key is to spend unstructured time with your children. You must realize that before you can effectively communicate with one another, you must spend time together. Teenagers often clam up during a scheduled, face-to-face talk. During less formal interaction, however, they really begin to open up, because the pressure to communicate is lifted. Examples of unstructured time include enjoying a meal together, driving to an event together, or even standing in a fast-food line together.

Occasions such as these provide great opportunities to ask your teen questions she might not answer during a more structured time together. Often kids will begin to open up to you during spontaneous moments because they do not feel any pressure from you. No pressure, combined with no demands, makes for intense communication. Spending unstructured time with your teenager will enable you to share the Lord with her in an unpressured atmosphere. It will also provide her with an honest view of your heart and help her understand your feelings on different issues and life situations.

In Deuteronomy 6:7–9, God tells us how to instill godly character into our children during the unstructured or everyday moments of life. We are to repeat His commands to our children again and again—to talk about them when we're at home and when we're away on a journey, when we're lying down and when we're getting up again. We are to tie them around our hands as a reminder and wear them on our foreheads. God tells us to write them on the doorposts of our houses and on our gates. God's Word is not just something you talk about when you go to church on Sunday. This commandment requires a continual act of building character in your children and letting them see the importance of a relationship with their heavenly Father.

It's important to set aside recreational time with your teen, to get involved with things she enjoys. You should encourage her to participate in activities you like such as shopping, going to the movies, playing golf, or water-skiing. Going on recreational trips together can facilitate an incredible time of bonding.

The other day, as I boarded an airplane, I started talking to a man who had raised five extremely successful children. Three of them were Harvard-graduate doctors and lawyers. I asked him how he was able to do that in today's world. He responded that he had the best backyard in the whole neighborhood. All the kids came to his house to spend the night. He didn't let his kids spend the night at other people's houses because he didn't have control over what went on in their homes. But as long as they were at his house, he could control the things they watched and discussed. He could ensure that the atmosphere and influence stayed positive rather than negative.

Parents also need to spend casual time together. It can be an excellent time of sharing with one another from the heart. During such moments, you will have the opportunity to discuss developments in your teenager's life and agree on the best course of action for her.

The second key to successful parenting is to start disciplining your child while she is still young. Parents need to agree on the best type of discipline for their children, taking into account that each one is an individual. An especially sensitive child, realizing that she has disappointed you, might break into tears if looked at the wrong way. Another one of your children might require quite a bit more discipline, making you question whether you even got through. The important thing is that you agree on the type of discipline each child needs and enforce it together. Both parents, rather than just one of them, should be disciplinarians.

Third, parents should team up together to show appreciation for their teenager. They can do things like drive their teen to places she can't reach on foot, give her little notes of heartfelt appreciation, or buy her small gifts they know she will enjoy. Doing these types of things will let her know they care for and love her. First Thessalonians 5:12–13 says we are to appreciate those who diligently labor among us. Our teens are no exception to this rule. We need to show them appreciation when we see them doing things that please us. Don't just correct them when they do something wrong. Praise them when you see them doing the right thing.

Finally, you need to verbally express your love to your child. It's amazing how many teens desire to have their parents look them in the eye and tell them they love them. It's also amazing how few parents actually do it. Several years ago when we were youth pastors, my wife, Angel, put her arm around one of the girls in the church and told her she loved her. When the girl began to sob, my wife asked her why she was crying. To Angel's surprise, the girl replied that nobody had ever told her they loved her. That meant that none of her family members, including her mom and dad, had ever told her they loved her. My wife's expression of love had such a profound effect on that young woman that she decided to become a missionary. To this day she remains a very close friend of our family.

In addition to showing your teenager love, you need to show affection toward each other as parents. Your child will someday look for those same responses and attitudes in a mate. She is watching you to see the way you react to one another. Your home should be a place of fun, encouragement, and positive reinforcement for all who live there, including the parents.

Affirmation: *I thank You, Lord, that _____(name of spouse) and I are working together as a team to raise up our child in the way she should go. Thank You for showing us the best form of discipline for our child, one that she will respond to positively and quickly. Our child is secure in the fact that we love her and therefore enjoys spending time with us.*

Affirmation Scriptures:
Ephesians 6:4; Proverbs 22:6; Proverbs 3:12; and Malachi 4:6.

17

Keeping Control Through Communication

ONE OF THE MOST important ingredients to a successful family is good communication among the members. Although open communication with your teen is important, it is equally, if not more, important to communicate effectively with your spouse. Occasionally teenagers will pit one spouse against the other in order to get their own way—the old "divide and conquer" method. Parents need to operate in agreement and communicate effectively with one another to prevent a teen from dividing them. If your teen believes he can obtain his own personal goals by manipulating and dividing you as his parents, he may plant a seed of disunity that, if unchecked, will eventually destroy both your marriage and family.

God's design for the home focuses on parents first and children second. All too often, that order becomes reversed and results in child-centered rather than parent-centered families. Genesis 2:24 says, "Therefore a man shall leave his father and mother and be joined to his wife, and they shall become one flesh" (NKJV). How many times have you heard someone ask newly married couples, "So, when are you going to start your family?" According to biblical standards, however, the basic family unit is comprised of husband and wife rather than parent and child. You and your spouse form a family from the moment you are joined in holy matrimony, regardless of whether or not you have any children.

As with all major parenting issues, parents need to be in agreement on decisions involving discipline and the drawing of boundary lines for their teenager. It's all too easy for parents to fall into the "good guy vs. bad guy" approach to parenting. In a home of this type, the father might always be the bad guy or disciplinarian who says no, while the mother is the buddy or nurturer. The reverse may also be true.

The danger presented by disagreement on parenting issues can be seen clearly in the family of "Charles" and "Shelly," parents of a teenage daughter in Detroit, Michigan. This family exemplified the good guy vs. bad guy approach to parenting.

Shelly, seeking to establish a relationship with her daughter based upon friendship, wound up neglecting her role as mother. With her words, she effectively undermined all behavioral parameters drawn for their daughter. She said things to her daughter like, "Your father doesn't want you out past eleven o'clock," or "Your dad found out you were dating so-and-so, and he doesn't like it," or "Your father is tired of walking into your bedroom and finding your room a mess." She always pointed the finger at the dad when it came to issues involving limitations or discipline. At the same time, she sympathized with her daughter by saying things such as, "I think that boy you're dating is okay," or "I don't think your room is that dirty." She was trying to make her daughter into her ally.

In the long run, this behavior eroded the marriage relationship between the father and mother. It also caused her relationship with her daughter to change from parent-child to buddy-buddy. Eventually, the daughter refused to receive any instruction or correction from her mother.

It wasn't until the daughter took off on a weekend excursion with her new boyfriend that the parents woke up and realized things had to change. Through prayer and the straightening of their priorities, they chose to form a family consisting of husband and wife first, parents and children second. Their daughter was therefore brought into an already solidly formed family consisting of husband and wife. The parents began to agree with each other on decision making, instruction, and discipline. It took some time, but eventually God worked out their relationship with one another.

It is critical not to allow a parent-child alliance to divide the parent-parent relationship. Permitting your child to divide and conquer will not only hurt your marriage, but it will also destroy the security of your home. A good, strong relationship between you and your spouse, based on effective communication and agreement on parenting decisions, will put your home on a firm foundation and breed security in your teenager.

Affirmation: *Father, I thank You that our home is built upon Your Word and Your ordained order. My spouse and I refuse to be divided on decisions involving the discipline of, or drawing of parameters for, our teen. Our teen is secure in knowing that our home is built on the firm foundation of a strong marriage between his parents.*

Affirmation Scriptures:
2 Corinthians 13:11; James 1:19; Philippians 2:2;
and Ephesians 3:17–18.

18

Parents' Influence over Their Teenagers

PARENTS MUST REALIZE that the goal in parenting is not so much to control their teenager as it is to influence her in making correct decisions. As a parent, God has given you the responsibility of training up your child, teaching her to make sound decisions, based on godly principles, that will last a lifetime. You need to train her not only in the art of making decisions, but also in walking out those decisions with integrity and purity. Remember that you won't always be making decisions for her. She must understand that if she makes bad decisions, she will experience the negative consequences of those choices. As a parent, you have the opportunity to make a lasting impression (whether favorable or unfavorable) on your child. That is why Proverbs 22:6 says, "Train up a child in the way he should go,/ And when he is old he will not depart from it" (NKJV). Notice the Scripture says "train" up a child rather than "raise" up a child.

In the United States, we often think that if we just feed our kid, send her off to school, and drop her off at church for an hour or two a week, she will turn out all right. We expect the youth pastor to wave his magic wand over our child during those two hours a week and transform her into some incredibly obedient and successful person. But God says it is *our* responsibility to do the actual training of our child. The Bible instructs us in Proverbs 22:6 to "teach your children to choose the right path, and when they are older, they will remain upon it" (NLT). Not only are we to teach them how to make right decisions, but we are also to show them how to stand upon and walk out those decisions.

When a person reaches adolescence, she experiences four basic changes in her life. The first change is physical, when a child "moves in to" an adult's body. This includes the coming alive of glands and hormones that dramatically affect the behavior, moods, and attitudes of teenagers.

The second is social change, where peer relationships become much more influential than they were before adolescence. Peer influence seems to play a greater role in families where the teen failed to bond well with her parents during early childhood years.

The next basic transition involves spiritual change. The teenager begins to discover her own spirituality. She ceases to rely primarily on her parents' spiritual experience and begins to feel the need to have her own experiences and encounters with God. That is why it's so important for you to pray that God would reveal Himself to your teen during this period of development. You need to pray as Paul prayed in Ephesians: that God would open the eyes of her understanding; and that she would know the hope of her calling, the riches of her inheritance in the saints, and the greatness of God's power focused toward us who believe (see Eph. 1:18–19 NKJV).

The last basic change that a child experiences upon reaching adolescence is the discovery of her gifts and talents. Parents play a major role in this fourth basic change in a child's life. The Amplified Version of Proverbs 22:6 says, "Train up a child in the way he should go (and in keeping with his individual gift or bent), and when he is old he will not depart from it." One of the most influential aspects of training up your child is showing her the gifts and talents God has placed in her life. This will help your child discover her destiny, and in doing so, she will not depart from it. Providing her with a purpose for living will cause her to understand that a divine calling is much more than just a vocation. It is a God-given purpose for "such a time as this."

The most successful, disciplined teenagers I have ever met are those with a goal and a purpose. They *know* the direction in which they are going. When a teenager has no direction, she only goes through the motions of life, getting off track and becoming rebellious. But when a teen's mind is filled with destiny, she'll begin to develop and exercise the gifts and talents God has already placed in her life. She'll take steps to become a positive influence on her peers.

Let us look at the example of "Amy," a good girl from Washington State who never seemed to get in much trouble. When Amy reached her teenage years, however, her parents noticed that her attitude began to erode. She started hanging around the wrong group of people, who exerted a negative influence over her life. I encouraged Amy's parents to discover some of her gifts and talents and to foster the development of those talents. Several months later, they came back and said they could not believe the transformation that had taken place in their daughter. She had become focused, more alive, and more attentive in developing her gifts and fulfilling her God-given destiny.

As a parent, you can have more influence over your teenager than can any other person—especially when it comes to developing the gifts and talents God has deposited in her life. Your job as a parent is to discover those gifts and aim your child in the right direction, training her up in accordance with those gifts and calling.

Affirmation: *Father, I thank You that I am a godly and favorable influence on my child. I train up my child in the way she should go, and she does not depart from it. My child makes good decisions and walks out those choices with integrity and determination. She recognizes the gifts and talents God has placed in her life and unswervingly pursues her God-given destiny with persistence and faith.*

Affirmation Scriptures:
Proverbs 22:6; Romans 8:14; Psalm 32:8; and Romans 8:28.

19

Sibling Relationships and Your Teenager

"CONCERNING BROTHERLY LOVE you have no need that I should write to you, for you yourselves are taught by God to love one another" (1 Thess. 4:9 NKJV). God's Word repeatedly teaches that we are to love and hold dear those people with whom we are in lifelong relationship. This includes our spouse, parents, brothers, sisters, etc.

It also tells us that we learn to manage greater responsibilities by handling lesser ones right now (see Matt. 25:21). Applying this principle to relationships, we can say that the way we treat our siblings while growing up is often the way we will treat others (such as our spouse, friends, and neighbors) who become a part of our adult lives. Are we quick to forgive, or do we hold grudges? Are we cynical, or are we encouraging? Do we find fault with other people, or do we always believe the best in others? Sibling relationships develop character traits in us that will affect us the rest of our lives. As parents, we have the ability to create a family environment conducive to developing unity and teamwork in our children rather than division and competition.

Parents can do a number of things to ensure that their children develop healthy sibling relationships. First, do not fall into the trap of comparing your children to each other. Statements like "Why can't you be more like your brother?" or "Your sister never gives me these problems" cause competition. Rather than helping them work together, it will foster strife and encourage a negative and combative view of their siblings. As a parent, you must realize that God made each one of your children to be an individual. No two of them will ever be the same. One may be a straight-A student and a bookworm, while another may have incredible people skills.

The second thing you can do to encourage healthy sibling relationships is put a stop to "cut downs." Colossians 4:6 says, "Let your speech always be with grace, seasoned with salt, that you may know how you ought to answer each one" (NKJV). Negative words can have a profound effect on your teen, especially if those words come from a brother or sister or from a parent. Such words can dramatically lower a child's self-esteem. If you allow your children to criticize and condemn each other, it will affect the relationships they form later on down the road. There really is something to the old saying "If you can't say something nice, don't say anything at all." Grandmother knew what she was talking about!

Key number three is to be an example. Siblings often mirror their parents' marriage relationship. If parents participate in coarse jesting and criticism, siblings will also tease and criticize each other. On the other hand, if parents affirm one another, siblings will often reflect that same attitude with their brothers and sisters.

Key number four: Teach your children to encourage one another. If you see that one of your kids is going through a difficult time, pull his brothers and sisters aside and let them know their sibling really needs the family's support. Urge them to find something good or affirming to say about him. Through teaching your children to encourage each other, you will profoundly affect not only the child who needs support, but also the brothers and sisters who give it.

Fifth, show them how to negotiate rather than fight. Don't allow your children to hit or beat up each other. Make your children sit down and talk through their disagreements. If they can't do it themselves, one of the parents should act as an arbiter between the two quarreling children, helping them to work things out and communicate with one another. Such negotiation skills, acquired while they are young, will serve them for the rest of their lives. What better place to start developing these skills than with their own brothers and sisters.

Next, teach your child to take responsibility for his actions. You can teach this principle most effectively through your own example. When you make a mistake, own up to it. Admit you are wrong without trying to blame your conduct on someone else. The Bible teaches us that we are all accountable for our own sins, regardless of the wrongful acts committed by others (see Rom. 14:10–13). Children must learn not to blame others for their mistakes, but to take responsibility for their actions.

We also need to ensure that our children understand they are not responsible for the behavior of their brothers and sisters. Be careful not to blame your older children for the behavior of their younger siblings. It is all too easy to single out one particular child on which to blame every squabble. Eventually this child will take on an attitude of guilt regardless of whether he actually did wrong.

Finally, you must deal with any bad attitudes your children may have. Parents should not ignore wrong thinking on the part of their kids by assuming it will go away on its own. You are not doing your teen any favors by failing to confront a poor outlook on others or on life in general. If you expose and correct wrong attitudes, you will do your child, as well as his future spouse and employees, a great service. By dealing with it now, you will help build character in his life. The fact is that attitude is extremely important. If you want the best for your child, you must teach him that his attitude is a primary contributor to his rate of success. Isaiah 1:19 says that if you are willing (which is your attitude) and obedient (which is your action), you will eat the good of the land. Action and attitude go hand-in-hand with success.

Affirmation: *My child is developing solid, loving relationships with his siblings. He seeks to build up and not to tear down his brothers and sisters.*

Because he approaches life from a godly, faith-filled perspective, he finds success in all his endeavors and relationships with others.

Affirmation Scriptures:

Colossians 4:6; Galatians 5:22–23; Romans 15:5–6; and Ephesians 4:2–3.

20

Protecting Your Teenager
from Outside Influences

PROTECTING YOUR TEENAGER from outside negative influences exerted through music, television, movies, or friends is a crucial part of training her up properly. All of these things have a profound impact on your teen, molding and influencing her personal attitudes and approach to life. You must realize that your role as a parent is not just to enforce rules. It also requires you to instill principles in her life that will help her make good decisions and accurately choose between right and wrong.

You need to be aware of the things in which your teenager is involved. Know what television shows she watches and what music she listens to. Find out what kind of posters she hangs on her walls and with what friends she hangs around. Then discuss all of these things with her. Remember the biblical principle of sowing and reaping. In Galatians 6:7 we are told that whatever we sow is what we will reap. Those things we put into our minds, our thinking, and our consciousness are what will come out of us in the end. To counteract negative influences and reinforce positive ones, parents must be aware of the things their teenagers put into their minds and consciousness.

There are several things you can do to help your child better discern the spiritual nature of those things she listens to or watches. Whatever she plants in her mind will eventually produce a harvest in her life, whether for good or for bad. The first thing you can do to help her is to spend time with her in activities such as attending church, playing games, fishing, camping, or shopping. After doing something with your teenager, talk to her about it—ask her what she liked or didn't like. Then ask her why she feels that way. And *listen* to her answer before responding. Make only comments that are nonthreatening.

Next, make it a point to meet her friends and have them come over to your house. Be warm and welcoming—talk to them, find out what they're like. Make your house into a fun place where teens feel welcome and have a variety of activities to do such as playing video games or pool. And make sure you have lots of food for them to eat! You may not always know what goes on at another person's house, but you do know what goes on at yours. Establish your home as a place of positive, rather than negative, influence.

Finally, if you go out to a movie with your teen or listen to music she enjoys, ask her some questions about it afterward. Get her to talk to you about the message of the song or movie, and ask her what she thought the writers were trying to get across to the audience. Doing this will cause her to consider more carefully what she takes into her life and what fruit it will produce.

Affirmation: *My teen accurately discerns the spiritual nature of those things in which she is involved or to which she listens. She makes good choices, effectively understanding the difference between right and wrong. As her parents, we provide a positive home environment for her and her friends to enjoy.*

Affirmation Scriptures:
Proverbs 2:10–15; Philippians 2:13; and 1 Thessalonians 5:22.

21

Helping Your Teen Choose Quality Friends

A RECENT SURVEY was taken of prison guards who worked in juvenile detention centers. When asked why so many young people wound up in youth prison facilities, they responded that it was because of older criminal influence. In their opinion, 100 percent of the teens and children incarcerated in detention centers had gotten their start in crime when someone older with criminal experience showed them how to steal or commit other illegal acts. Absent the influence of these older criminals, the officers were convinced that many young people might never have gone down the road to crime.

Friends are an important and influential part of your teenager's life. They play a major role in his progression from child to adult and influence him in ways that we can't. They help to form his understanding of who he is and what he will become. If we want to see our kids prosper in the Lord, we must first determine what type of friends we want them to have and then steer them in the right direction. We need to encourage them to form relationships with friends of good character and influence: "Don't be fooled by those who say such things, for 'bad company corrupts good character'" (1 Cor. 15:33 NLT).

In the Word, we see three different types of friends: unbelievers; lukewarm Christians, or "good" kids; and sold-out, on-fire believers. The first type of friend is described in the book of Corinthians: "Do not be unequally yoked together with unbelievers. For what fellowship has righteousness with lawlessness? And what communion has light with darkness?" (2 Cor. 6:14 NKJV).

This passage encourages us not to form strong friendships with unbelievers. It's difficult to walk closely with God if our friends want nothing to do with Him. This doesn't mean that our teenagers should avoid the unsaved as if they suffer from cooties or halitosis. Rather, it means that their closest friends, those who comprise their inner circle, should be born-again, on-fire Christians. In other words, it's okay to be friendly with people in the world; just don't form close bonds of mutual influence with them.

Even Christian friends can exert a negative influence if they aren't on fire for Jesus! At times, this type of influence can be the most detrimental because it tends to sneak up on us. Before we know it, such friends have altered our way of thinking and doused some of our fire for God: "You were running well; who hindered you from obeying the truth? This persuasion did not come from Him who calls you. A little leaven leavens the whole lump of dough" (Gal. 5:7–9 NASB).

The influence of leaven can be difficult to detect at first. This type of friend is usually what people call a good kid. They are the school football stars, cheerleaders, and straight-A students. They faithfully attend church and appear to be good kids on the outside. But I have known some good, churchgoing teens who smoked pot in a cornfield and partied behind their parents' backs, dragging plenty of other teens along with them. Generally, teenagers either serve God with all their hearts or they wind up getting into some kind of trouble. There really isn't any in-between today.

The third type of friend is the one who encourages your teenager to serve God and draw closer to Him. These friends are true believers:

And let us consider one another in order to stir up love and good works, not forsaking the assembling of ourselves together, as is the manner of some, but exhorting one another, and so much the more as you see the Day approaching. (Heb. 10:24–25 NKJV)

Developing friendships with this caliber of person will challenge your teen to grow in his personal relationship with God. Every time he gets together with them, they will inspire him to do more, and be more, for Jesus. We must get a vision and believe God to bring this type of friend into our children's lives. If there are none in sight, get down and pray, believing God to do it. It's not enough to avoid negative influences; we must go for God's best—radical, on-fire, Jesus-loving friends.

One of the most important ways that parents can help their teens choose quality friends is to be involved in their lives. Don't send your child down to Johnny's house without first knowing something about Johnny. You have the right to ask questions and find out more about your child's friends. Remember that he is still a teenager and not an adult. Parents have the God-given responsibility to assist their children in selecting friends. Although your teenager may not appreciate the prying and may protest that you are invading his space, do not give up. He needs your input whether he acknowledges it or not.

Get to know the parents of your child's friends. Volumes can be learned from just a simple telephone call. By getting to know the parents, you can also learn something about the kids. You will have more opportunity to observe the type of families from which they come. This in turn will help you to determine what kind of environment your teen is exposed to whenever he goes to their houses.

Make sure you communicate the advantages of hanging around with kids of high moral standards. Allow your teenager extra privileges when he goes out with this type of friend. Let him stay out later, spend the night, or enjoy some other kind of special privilege. If he hangs out with teens of less positive influence, be sure to place safe and healthy limits on how he spends time with them.

Reach out to the families of the teenagers with whom you want your child to become friends. Plan family outings together and develop a relationship with their parents. By becoming friends with the entire family, you will help strengthen the bonds of friendship between them.

You should also try to monitor the age of your teen's friends. If he is easily influenced, encourage him to develop friendships with kids his age or younger. You do not want him to hang around older teenagers because they may exert undue influence on him. Remember when your children were little tykes running around on the playground? If your kid allowed Biff the Bully to drag him around by the ear, he is probably a follower and thus more likely to be influenced by his friends. If, on the other hand, your child resembled Sammy the Drill Sergeant and bossed all the other kids around, he is probably more of a leader and not so easily influenced.

Supervise his activities with friends. Certain types of immoral behavior require both time and privacy to accomplish. Your teen can still have his space without it being too private. This is what I call being alone in a public place. It may be in your backyard, living room, or a public restaurant. Because he is never completely alone with a member of the opposite sex, it allows him to get to know them without placing himself in a position of temptation. Watching your child interact with his friends will also enable you to observe their character qualities firsthand.

You may feel that you are being too intrusive, but let me encourage you to trust your instincts. Remember that the Holy Spirit is there to help you. When small signs of trouble crop up, it usually indicates the existence of a greater problem behind the facade. Don't be afraid to follow through with what God has placed in your heart.

Sally was riding the fence and living on the edge of trouble. She had started to date and was spending time with some good church kids who did not seem to be as interested in God as they were in her. Although her parents were not happy with the direction she was heading, they were not sure how to handle it. Some advised that she would only rebel if they tightened the reins on her. Others told her parents to do whatever was necessary to get her back on the right path.

Her parents decided to do two very important things. Number one, they immediately cut off all apparent negative influences. At first, this was not much fun. She screamed, tried to sneak out of the house, and did everything in her power to turn the home into a WWF wrestling ring.

The second thing they did was to spend more time with her and schedule more family activities. These family outings served to replace some of the teen-only events with which she had been previously involved. Although this transition took time, it was well worth the effort. That young girl was saved a tremendous amount of heartache, all because her parents became involved in her life. Enrolled in a school of ministry, she is now preparing for full-time gospel work.

Parents have the ability to influence their children's decisions concerning friends. It is a simple principle: Whoever has the strongest relationship with your child will also have the greatest influence on him. In 1960, teenagers were polled to determine what type of people and things influenced them the most. Out of choices such as music, television, parents, pastors, and sports stars, the number-one influence in teens' lives was parents.

They administered this same poll again in 1980 to see how things had changed. In the new poll, teens ranked their parents below things like television stars, music, and friends. Pollsters concluded that parents were spending less time with their children and had lost important ground in their relationship with their teenagers. This accounted for the loss of parental influence in their lives. Parents can win back the ability to be heard by their teenagers if they are willing to spend more time with them. Then they will be able to influence their teens' choice of friends.

Finally, seek to develop in him an appreciation for quality friends. Discuss with your teenager how friends can either hinder his walk with God or spur him on to greater heights. Examine the characteristics of a true friend who "sticks closer than a brother" (Prov. 18:24 NKJV). Encourage him to seek out friends who will challenge him to go on with God and grab hold of his destiny.

Friends can influence us for good or for evil. They have the capacity to spur us on to greater glory in God or to drag us down to the pit. Parents need to be involved with their teenagers, helping them to select godly friends. By doing so, parents will positively impact their teens' choice of friends and help protect them from destructive influences.

Affirmation: *My teen chooses only quality friends who love God and encourage him to be sold out for Jesus. He is challenged to grow in his personal relationship with God. As his parent, I seek to help him form godly friendships with young people of good character and influence.*

Affirmation Scriptures:
Proverbs 13:20; 2 Timothy 2:22; Proverbs 2:20; and Psalm 1:1–3.

22

Training Up Your Child

ONE OF THE MOST widely quoted verses in the Bible as applied to child-rearing can be found in Proverbs 22:6: "Train up a child in the way he should go, / And when he is old he will not depart from it" (NKJV). Why does it seem as though so many teenagers have departed from the way in which their parents trained them? I'm sure you've heard this scenario before: Two godly parents successfully raise their well-behaved child in a good family—until their child becomes a teenager. Whammo! All of a sudden, their little angel becomes Beelzebub. It appears as though their once obedient child made a 180-degree turn from the way she was brought up.

Proverbs 22:6 is probably one of the most misinterpreted verses in the entire Bible. A lot of people mistakenly read it as follows: Train up a child in the way he should go by pointing out all his flaws and telling him to do this and not to do that, and he will not depart from it. A closer look at this verse in the Amplified Version, however, enables us to see that it is when we properly train up a child *in keeping* with his individual gifts or bent that he will not depart from it.

It is essential for parents, youth leaders, and all persons of influence in a teenager's life to discover the gifts and personal interests of that teenager and aim her in the right direction. As you aim your teen toward her individual calling and gifts, she will not depart from that direction. Helping your teenager gain a vision for her life is one of the most important things you can do for her. Although she may have incredible talent in the areas of art, music, administration, or leadership, your teen may never realize her gifts if you don't tell her; she is so familiar with her gift that she doesn't consciously recognize its existence. If you see your teenager doing something outstanding, let her know what an incredible job she did. You will be amazed at how surprised she is when you compliment her work. Hanging over her shoulder, you comment on her beautiful artwork, and all she can say is "Really?" She is essentially clueless about the value of her gift because it comes naturally to her.

Your job as a parent is to help train up your child, encouraging her to excel in those gifts and inclinations placed within her by God. That is why it is essential to major on the good things your child does and only minor on what she does wrong. Doing this will produce confidence and faith in her.

Affirmation: *I thank You, Father, for helping me to aim my child in the direction of Your gifts and calling on her life. She is walking in the pursuit of that calling and does not depart from it. Thank You, Lord, for showing her the value of her God-given gifts and talents.*

Affirmation Scriptures:
Proverbs 22:6; Deuteronomy 28:3, 6; Isaiah 54:13; and Ephesians 6:4.

23

Teaching Your Child to Dream

ONE OF THE MOST important things you can do as a parent is to point your teenager toward God's vision and purpose for his life. Letting your child know that he was not an accident, but was preordained by God to be born at such a time as this, will give him a powerful sense of purpose for his life.

Some time ago, a child psychologist asked me what I thought was the major problem among teenagers today. Turning the question back on him, I asked what he thought it was. Without a moment's hesitation, he responded that it was a lack of discipline. The more I thought about his statement, the more I concluded that a lack of discipline is merely a symptom of something else. It results from a lack of vision. Proverbs 29:18 says, "Where there is no vision, the people perish" (KJV). Other versions say that where there is no vision, the people "cast off restraint" (NIV), "run wild" (TLB), are "unrestrained" (NASB). One of the primary reasons teenagers run wild today, unrestrained and without self-discipline, is because they have no vision for their lives.

One of the things I love most about teenagers and about working with them is that they are so idealistic. The words "I can" seem to permeate their entire vocabulary. They are just radical enough to believe that they can do it if they can dream it. As parents, we often try to protect our children from hurt or disappointment. In doing so, however, we prevent them from dreaming big dreams and frustrate creative or imaginative thinking on their parts. We must understand that vision comes before discipline. Discipline, absent the motivation presented by vision, will quickly turn into legalism.

Years ago when I was a youth pastor, I knew a newly saved Christian who lacked any revelation of personal hygiene. He seemed to be contaminated with bad breath and body odor. I tried so hard to work with this young man, to help him clean himself up and take pride in his appearance. But he never seemed to catch on. Then one day in youth group I noticed that he was bathed, his hair and teeth were brushed, and he even had on cologne. I thought, "Thank God this guy finally caught on to what I've been telling him." Well, I found out that he had come in contact with what one man called a "UFO," an unidentified female object. He caught a vision of himself together with this young woman and realized he would have to take better care of himself to make it happen. It gave him a reason to tuck in his shirttail, brush his hair and teeth, and clean himself up. First comes vision. Then comes discipline.

Parents need to become dream builders and not dream wreckers for their children. If you overhear your teenager telling you what he would like to do or accomplish in life, encourage him in it. Be sure not to discourage him from pursuing the dreams and desires God has placed within his heart.

Affirmation: *Thank You, heavenly Father, that my child has a vision for his life. He dreams big dreams and knows that he can accomplish them through the help of Your Holy Spirit. I commit myself to help him realize those goals and to foster a sense of divine purpose in him.*

Affirmation Scriptures:
Jeremiah 29:11; Joel 2:28; Proverbs 29:18; and Philippians 4:13.

24

Helping Your Child Discover His Calling

ONE OF THE GREATEST discoveries a person can ever make is to find his God-given calling. Sometimes this can be one of the most difficult things to do. Parents can help their children discover their calling, especially during their formative teenage years. To do this, you must first help your child discover his heart's desires. Next, you need to help him ascertain his God-given abilities. Notice what comes easily to him, those things in which he excels. Finally, encourage him in his gifts and talents. Remember that it's not your responsibility to create a destiny for him—God has already done that. You just need to be there to help him discover that destiny. Understand that you're not alone in training up your child. God is also at work in him.

Through my study of the Scriptures, I have discovered that God reveals our divine destiny through two primary avenues. Philippians 2:13 says, "For it is God who works in you both to will and to do for His good pleasure"(NKJV). This verse sets forth a twofold plan of action. First, God works in us "to will." That means He is placing His desires and His will into our hearts. The second part of that Scripture tells us that He is also working in us "to do" of His good pleasure. That says He is placing in us the abilities, the talents, and the gifts necessary to fulfill our God-given purpose here on earth.

As a parent, you need to get involved with your teenager in order to understand the nature of his desires. I have discovered three major

63

things parents can do to discern their children's true aspirations. I call them the three Ts: what they spend their *time* on, what they *talk* about, and what they *think* about. When you put these three Ts together, you will have an accurate perception of their heart's desires. Parents should help their children discern their God-given desires, being careful not to impose the parents' ambitions on the children.

Someone once said that it would be a bummer to go through life climbing up the ladder of success only to get to the top and realize your ladder was leaned against the wrong building. I believe that as long as you have air in your lungs, it's not too late to rush down the ladder, find the right building, move your ladder onto that building, and start climbing up again. But how much better it is to climb up the right building from the start.

Not too long ago, I met a woman who spent her entire life working as a doctor only to realize at the age of fifty that she never really enjoyed doing it. She loved selling real estate and helping other people purchase the homes of their dreams. Upon discovering her true vocation, she changed professions and is now one of the top realtors in her region. She absolutely loves it. When asked why she spent the first half of her life doing something she didn't like, she smiled and replied, "Because I had ambitious parents."

Affirmation: *Father, I thank You that my teen has a solid understanding of the desires and abilities You have placed in him. Not only does he have a solid grasp of what those desires and abilities consist of, he also desires above all else to walk in them, to fulfill the destiny You created for him. As his parents, we seek to encourage him in his calling, to help him reach his full potential in Christ.*

Affirmation Scriptures:
Philippians 2:13; Jeremiah 29:13; Romans 8:14; and Psalm 31:3.

25

Helping Your Child Develop Her God-Given Gifts

NOTHING IS MORE rewarding to parents than watching their child blossom and flourish in her gifts and divine calling. Parents can assist their teen in developing those gifts, once they have been discerned. Proverbs 15:2 says that the tongue of the wise makes knowledge acceptable. It is one thing to simply spew out knowledge; it is another thing to make that knowledge so acceptable and appealing that your child can receive and digest it. Making your words more palatable will help you better reach her with sound advice and wisdom on the best way to develop her talents and abilities.

The following four keys will help you encourage development of your teen's God-given gifts. First, speak supportive words over her, words of affirmation and inspiration. The Bible instructs us to "encourage each other and build each other up, just as you are already doing" (1 Thess. 5:11 NLT). Encouragement of their child is the parents' full-time job, especially if condemnation and inferiority are bombarding the teen on a regular basis. Stop for a moment and think about the most positive influence in your life. Regardless of whether that person was a teacher, parent, pastor, or something else, I can promise you this: That person was an encourager. Ephesians 4:29 says, "Let no corrupt word proceed out of your mouth, but what is good for necessary edification, that it may impart grace to the hearers" (NKJV).

We need to edify and build up others with the words we speak.

Remember that everyone needs to be encouraged. No matter how confident your teenager may appear, she still needs edification. Words of affirmation do something supernatural, literally imparting grace to the listener. The term *grace* as used in Ephesians 4:29 is taken from the Greek root word *chairo,* meaning "to be cheerful or well off and full of joy."[1] Now, we know that joy produces strength, and the joy of the Lord is our strength. That is the reason you need to keep words of edification, exhortation, and affirmation flowing out of your mouth toward your teenager.

The second thing you can do is put your teen in situations where she has the opportunity to observe others exercising those same gifts. The Bible speaks of not letting knowledge depart from your eyes (Prov. 3:21). Watching someone else using similar gifts and talents in a way that blesses others can be very moving. I remember the first time I ever saw a gifted evangelist give an altar call. I was so captivated by the whole experience, including the response of the people, that it changed my life. I thought, *This is what I am going to be doing for the rest of my life.* Bringing a piano player to watch a gifted pianist perform at a concert will move and inspire him. In the same way, placing your teenager in situations where she can observe the exercise of similar gifts will encourage and inspire her.

A third way to help her develop her talents is to introduce her to other people with the same gifts. It will greatly encourage your teenager to be able to sit down and talk with other people who are currently moving in gifts closely paralleling her own. It will also provide her with the opportunity to ask questions of and "touch" someone who is already utilizing abilities your teenager desires to develop. She will be able to learn from their backgrounds and from the obstacles they had to overcome to get to where they are now.

The fourth key in helping your teen develop her talents and abilities is the availability of resources. Make important resources available to her through books and articles on her gifts and calling, biographies, interviews, Web pages, and videos. Each of these things will encourage your teenager to go after the vision and calling of God with passion and persistence.

Affirmation: *My teen walks in the divine calling and gifts of God. Watching others follow in similar callings motivates and encourages her to develop her own gifts and talents. We support and encourage her through our words and actions, helping her to unswervingly pursue the call of God on her life.*

Affirmation Scriptures:

1 Thessalonians 5:11; 1 John 2:27; Luke 4:18; and Jeremiah 1:5.

26

All Teenagers Are Created Equal, but Not All Are Created Alike

ONE OF THE MOST exciting things about God is that He created every person to be an individual, with unique gifts and callings. The sad thing is that, after graduating from college, so many people are willing to sacrifice their individuality and become clones of someone else. God has not called us to be clones. He has called us to be individuals conformed to the image of Christ and walking in our unique gifts and callings.

God has given parents special influence with their teenagers to help them develop their talents. We can actually encourage our children to be individuals. This in turn will enhance the growth of their gifts.

There are three basic things parents can do to foster the development of their teenagers as individuals. First, don't compare them to other people. They will do enough of that on their own. Next, help them discover their special gifts and then affirm them in those gifts. Finally, encourage your children to give themselves entirely over to those God-given gifts.

Second Corinthians 10:12 says that when we compare ourselves with one another, we are without understanding. One of the reasons comparison can be so devastating is that it limits personal growth and development. When we compare ourselves to somebody else, we can only become as good as the people to whom we are comparing. That's why Jesus said that a disciple is not above his teacher and a servant will never be better than his master.

When I first got started in ministry, I remember walking on the golf course at night, praying and thinking about all my heroes of faith. I began to think about the apostle Paul and the revealed knowledge in which he walked. Then my thoughts turned to a preacher named Billy Sunday and his success in communicating the gospel. I thought about Billy Graham and how many souls he has led to Christ. Finally, I thought of Smith Wigglesworth and all the lives he had affected. Rather than become encouraged, I became discouraged because I began to compare myself to them. Then the Holy Spirit said something to my heart that radically changed me. He told me, "I don't need another apostle Paul; I've already had one. I don't need another Billy Sunday, Smith Wigglesworth, or Billy Graham because I've already had them too." He said, "I need an Eastman Curtis."

And that is exactly what God says about you and your teenager. He has created each one of us to be an individual with special gifts and callings for such a time as this. When we ask our child questions like "Why can't you be more like your brother?" or "Why couldn't you be more like your sister?" we destroy his sense of uniqueness.

The second way to encourage your children in their individual development is to help them discover their special gifts and then affirm the reality of those gifts. When our son was little, he liked to color pictures and hold them up for us to see. We would cut loose and praise him *big time*, telling him how great they looked. But as he got older, we stopped paying so much attention to things like that. Instead of praising him, we just sort of looked over the top of the newspaper, grunted out "pretty good," and then got back to the paper. We need to show the same, if not more, enthusiasm about the things our children do as they continue to grow older. If a teenager cannot get affirmation from his parents, he will find other places where he can. And all too often he will end up getting it from people and places not to his parents' liking.

First Corinthians 12:12 tells us, "The body is one and has many members, but all the members of that one body, being many, are one body, so also is Christ" (NKJV). God is telling us that each member of His body is a unique person. The eye functions differently than does the ear. The ear functions differently than the mouth. But they all work together. We cannot say that one member is more valuable or less valuable than the other members. One of your children may have great academic ability and graduate magna cum laude from college. Another child, however, may not do so well academically, but may have the managerial skills to run an entire corporation. One is not greater than the other. They are just different.

Third, you need to encourage your teenager to give himself entirely over to his God-given gifts. First Timothy 4:14–15 says, "Do not neglect the gift that is in you" but "meditate on these things; give yourself entirely to them, that your progress may be evident to all" (NKJV). As you encourage your teenager to meditate upon his gift and to give himself to it, his progress will be apparent to all those around him. Progress is a God-given thing. God does not want us to stagnate or regress; He wants us to progress continually. When we meditate on our gifts and give ourselves over to them, we cause our gifts to develop and increase. The more we use our gifts, the more they will continue to grow.

Several years ago during the winter Olympics, I saw an interview with one of the young American gold medalists in ice-skating. The interviewer asked her what the most difficult thing was she had had to do to win the gold medal. She looked up with a smile and said, "It really wasn't the practicing, because I love ice-skating so much." But she said that when other girls were playing with Barbies, shopping, or talking about guys, she was thinking about how she could be a better ice-skater and practicing, in the rink or watching videos of other ice-skaters. Then she held up the gold medal, looked into the camera, and said, "But it's worth it." She went on to tell what an encouragement her parents had been to her, how they had supported and backed her in her goal to win a gold medal.

As a parent, you have a major role in shaping and developing your teenager's gifts and calling. Parents need to support their children in their individual talents. Affirm them in their achievements and avoid comparing them with others. By doing this, you will encourage them to give themselves over to the unique talents and callings God has placed on their lives, thus spurring them on to greater success.

Affirmation: *I encourage each one of my children to discover and develop his own unique talents and calling from God. Because God has created them to be individuals, I do not compare them with others. My children receive affirmation from their parents and do not feel the need to get support from other people or places of which we do not approve.*

Affirmation Scriptures:
1 Timothy 4:14–15; Luke 4:18; 2 Peter 1:3; and Jeremiah 1:5.

27

Building Confidence in Your Teenager

BASIC TRAINING in the military was an adventure. Their motto was, "Tear them down, to build them back up." And let me assure you, they seemed to be quite proficient at it. One week, they sent us out in the field to do training maneuvers for three days. It was cold and rainy, and all we had to keep us warm were our M16s. On our second day out, we had mail call. My father had sent my Bible to me in the mail. The sergeant thought it was a care package containing food that our entire squad would be able to consume during training maneuvers. While we were lined up in formation, the squad tore into it, discovering that it was a Bible instead. When they realized it didn't contain any food, they became disappointed and upset. Needless to say, I was in trouble. As punishment, I had to endure a barrage of insults and was required to do fifty-plus push-ups. All for getting a Bible in the mail.

At the time, I was embarrassed. And then I felt embarrassed for feeling embarrassed. That feeling, however, was quickly replaced by confidence when more than a dozen people said they could not believe how I had stood up for my faith in the middle of those field maneuvers. While I was going through it, I didn't feel very confident. I felt alone, isolated, and even embarrassed. But later on, that event produced an assurance and a confidence in me because I held my ground. I knew that I would stick to my guns no matter how isolated I felt.

Although your teen may not go through basic training in the

military, he will go through basic-training maneuvers in life. He may often feel alone and isolated, especially if he is suffering persecution for his faith at school. The difference is that you can be there to encourage him; he doesn't have to go through it alone. You can do things to build confidence in him and impart strength for him to stand his ground.

One way to build confidence in your teenager is to affirm him. Most parents tell their teenager what a loser he is, either through their words, their body language, or both. If he attempts to discuss his views and opinions with his parents, they fold their arms, roll their eyes, frown, and even interrupt him. With negative reinforcement like this, it's no wonder our teens act so insecure and indecisive around their friends.

You will be amazed at how asking your teen's opinion, whether you agree with it or not, will help to promote confidence in him. If our heavenly Father can listen to us, we can listen to our children too: "But God had listened to Abraham's request and kept Lot safe, removing him from the disaster" (Gen. 19:29 NLT).

Keep in mind that your teenager may use a few words or illustrations that have the potential to light your fuse. But don't react. Instead, make a decision to put a filter on your ears and on your mouth. Listen to what James 1:19 has to say about this: "Dear friends, be quick to listen, slow to speak, and slow to get angry" (NLT). All too often, it seems that we end up being slow to listen, quick to speak, and quick to get angry. Just the opposite of what the Word commands. We need to stop ourselves before we react. We need to get this right.

Showing enthusiasm for the things your child does is a powerful tool for building up his self-esteem. When we are enthusiastic about something, whether it be our faith, job, family, or even our hobbies, our enthusiasm becomes contagious and develops unyielding steadfastness in ourselves and those around us: "Your zeal has stirred up the majority" (2 Cor. 9:2 NKJV). You can actually stir up people by your own zeal and enthusiasm. Just remember that it has to start with you. When you're enthusiastic about something, other people will become excited about it too.

Encourage him to allow God's Word to be his source of confidence. If we derive our security from God's Word, it will help us live victorious lives, independent of our circumstances. If your teen can grasp this truth and apply it to his life, he will not lack confidence on any level. Just remember that this principle is *caught* more than it's *taught*. Our teens will learn this truth more through the example of our lives than through what we preach. When they see that we derive our confidence from God's Word and are not shaken because of circumstances, they will put their security in God as well.

We can feel secure even in the midst of tough times. In fact, it's in the midst of life's challenges that we need our confidence the most: "As for God, His way is perfect; / The word of the LORD is proven; / He is a shield to all who trust in Him" (Ps. 18:30 NKJV).

Encourage your teen to develop a close relationship with God. It is incredible how a relationship with our living, vibrant heavenly Father increases our level of confidence. Everything can be falling apart around us, and then He whispers, "Nothing is impossible for you, because I will never leave you or forsake you." I would not swap this relationship for anything: "Does your reverence for God give you no confidence? Shouldn't you believe that God will care for those who are upright?" (Job 4:6 NLT).

A true relationship with God will boost your teen's confidence like nothing else. He will have the security of knowing that God cares for all those who love Him and live godly lives. God will not let him down. Assured of God's help, he will be able to confront even the most difficult of life's challenges with confidence.

Remember that your teen needs you. He needs you to be there for him—encouraging, affirming, and showing enthusiasm for the things that matter most to him. He needs you to point the way to a strong relationship with God and remind him that he is never alone.

Affirmation: *I seek to build up my teen and not to tear him down. Because he walks in close fellowship with God, he is confident that God is watching over him, helping him and caring for him. I encourage him through my words and my actions, helping to build self-esteem and confidence in him. He knows that he is not alone.*

Affirmation Scriptures:
Philippians 4:13; Hebrews 10:35; Ephesians 3:12; and Jeremiah 29:11.

28

Helping Your Teen Pursue Her Destiny

HELPING YOUR TEEN discover and pursue her destiny is one of the most important things you will ever do as a parent. It will help her to avoid wasting years of her life frantically searching for God's will because she will already be headed on the correct path. "Seeding" your children today with thoughts of divine destiny will help ensure their success tomorrow. It will help them reach for the stars, dream big dreams, and do great things for God.

Psalm 37:4 tells us that "He shall give you the desires of your heart" (NKJV). This verse highlights two very important principles: First, the Spirit of God will "give," or place, the desires in your heart. Second, He will "give" those desires to you by bringing them to pass in your life. In other words, the gifts that God places in your life coincide with the desires that He places within your heart.

Often, people waste valuable time agonizing over whether a particular desire is from God or from the flesh. Some people struggle so much that they end up waiting on God their entire lives. We need to realize that although there is a time to wait, there is also a time for action.

If your teen understands her calling, it can help alleviate much of this internal struggle and give her the confidence to persevere when the going gets tough. God has placed parents in a special position to influence their children for good, to help them discover God's will for their lives and then pursue it. Through your support and guidance, you can encourage your teen to go for God's best and never settle for less.

Tell her that God believes in her! God has appointed her to a call that no one else can fulfill. And He is confident that your teenager will succeed. God has appointed her as an ambassador for Christ, to bring the light of God to a dark and dying world:

> "And now," said the Lord—the Lord who formed me from my mother's womb to serve him who commissioned me to restore to him his people Israel, who has given me the strength to perform this task and honored me for doing it! . . . "I will make you a Light to the nations of the world to bring my salvation to them too." (Isa. 49:5–6 TLB)

Jeremiah was just a young man when God called him and set him apart for a great work. The Word tells us that God appointed Jeremiah as His "spokesman to the world" (Jer. 1:5 TLB). Now that's a pretty amazing job title for a young man. In today's terms, that means he was God's special mouthpiece to the entire world. The fact that Jeremiah was young didn't lessen God's confidence that he could do the job. As parents, we need to realize that God has set our teenagers apart for a divine purpose, calling them into His service before they were even born.

The problem with so many of this generation is that they do not have a vision for their lives. And without a vision, the Bible tells us that people perish or cast off self-restraint (Prov. 29:18). If we can help our teenagers get a vision for their lives, we can help them develop the self-discipline needed to attain their goals. Because where vision exists, discipline follows.

We need to teach our teens to dream—to embrace the possibilities of the future. Dreaming too big is better than not dreaming at all. Think of it this way: If you shoot for the stars and only make it to the moon, at least you've gotten to the moon. But if you don't try to do anything, you will never even get off the earth. If our teens are ever going to fulfill God's call and bring forth fruit in line with God's plan, they must get a vision for their lives. Remember that the dreamers of today are the movers and shakers of tomorrow.

By nature, all children are dreamers. When we are young, our imaginations know no boundaries: A young boy, captivated by the presidential address on television, boldly proclaims, "I'm going to be president when I grow up." In the same way, a young girl hears the soul-gripping story of the evangelist Kathryn Kuhlman, and sets her own sights on someday becoming a powerful instrument of God. Children dream of greatness, with never a thought of forfeiting that dream. But as we grow up, the world and sometimes even the church push us down and cause us to abort our God-given dreams and visions. To prevent this from happening to your teen, you need to encourage her to gain a real vision for her life, to believe God for great things and to not give up.

Encourage your teenager to avoid the rut of routine. We all do things in life without thinking because we are locked into certain habits. Many people unconsciously cruise through life, never stopping to think about the direction they are heading. Then, twenty or thirty years later, they suddenly start to question how they got to where they find themselves. Instead of taking responsibility for the direction of their lives, they blame circumstances. As George Bernard Shaw once said,

> People are always blaming their circumstances for what they are. I don't believe in circumstances. The people who get on in this world are the people who get up and look for the circumstances they want, and, if they can't find them, *make them.*

Discover the gifts and talents in your children and then do everything you can to foster the development of those gifts. If your child has a talent in the area of music, sign her up for music lessons. If she is a scientist by nature, take her to science museums and encourage her to read scientific books and magazines. If she shows an interest in ministry, encourage her to get involved in leadership in her church youth group. Find out your child's talents and then help her develop those abilities.

Train her to follow her heart. Remember that God not only gives us the desires of our hearts, He also gives or places those desires within us. If we listen to our hearts, we will hear the voice of God whispering in our ears, revealing His plan for our lives.

Once your teen has heard from God, she needs to develop a plan to pursue her destiny. There is a lot of truth to the saying, "If you fail to plan, you plan to fail." Visions are enacted through tangible means. If your teenager wants to be a teacher or lawyer or engage in a profession requiring a college education, she should begin planning now by applying herself to her studies and putting away money for school. If she wants to be in ministry, she can begin setting her sights on a degree in biblical studies. Maybe she feels called to be an international evangelist—get her involved in teen missions. If she wants to be president, expose her to the world of politics. No dream, no vision, is too great for God.

Finally, teach her to persevere in pursuing her dream. I have heard the Christian life compared to a long-distance race. It's not to the sprinter that the trophy will go. Rather, it's to the runner who refuses to give up, the one who goes the distance. So many people start out with a lot of enthusiasm, but when the going gets tough, they quit. If your teenager wants to realize her dream, to see her destiny come to pass, she can't be a quitter. As her parent, you can encourage her to look past any challenges she may encounter, to look down the road and see the joy set before her. That will motivate her to persevere even when facing great challenges.

The richest place on the planet is not the diamond mines of South Africa or the oil fields of Kuwait. The richest place on the planet is the cemetery. In the cemetery, we bury inventions never produced, ideas and dreams never realized, and aspirations never pursued. Many take to the grave the most vibrant and explosive resource the world could ever know—God-given dreams and visions.

God has made us to be the directors, producers, scriptwriters, and stars of our own lives. We are the ones who will decide whether the movie of our life will be a smash or a flop. I encourage you to dream big enough to challenge your faith, to break out of the bonds of mediocrity and reach for the humanly impossible. That kind of dreaming is contagious!

Affirmation: *Thank You, Lord, that my teenager knows and understands the divine call You have placed on her life. Keeping her destiny ever before her, she makes appropriate plans to see those dreams become a reality. Confident of God's support, she doesn't give up when tough times come. Instead, she makes it her lifelong goal to pursue the call of God on her life. As her parent, I encourage her in that calling and foster the development of her God-given gifts and talents.*

Affirmation Scriptures:
Philippians 1:6; Habakkuk 2:2; Psalm 5:12; and Joel 2:28.

29

Motivating Your Teenager

"WORRY WEIGHS a person down; an encouraging word cheers a person up" (Prov. 12:25 NLT). God has given parents special influence with their teenagers—to encourage or discourage, to motivate or to exasperate. Everyone needs encouragement and motivation, from the small toddler on up to the senior citizen.

Let me give you a personal illustration of this truth. When my little girl was three years old, she grabbed me by the hand and brought me outside. She wanted me to swing her. But when I went to push her, she said, "No, Daddy. Don't push. Just stand over there and tell me how good I'm doing." Sometimes all our children need is for us to stand on the sidelines and cheer them on.

There are two types of motivation, internal and external. For instance, let's say that you have a teenager who makes Cs on his schoolwork. As his parent, you want to motivate him to pull those Cs up to As. Lots of parents might say to their teen, "No television until your grades are pulled up." They replace television watching with three hours of study every night. In all probability, your teenager won't be motivated to do much studying. In fact, if the parent is fortunate, the teenager might at least put up with that rule. But a true heart change is unlikely to result solely from external motivation.

I have found that internal motivation works more effectively with teenagers. Talk to your teenager about his goals and desires. You can do this while he's watching television, cleaning his room, or even drawing a picture. Then begin to ask him questions about how he plans to achieve his dreams and desires. As parents, we need to look for a spark of interest in our child and then fan that spark into flames. Within each person lies a dream given by the Holy Spirit. We just need to pick up on that spark of motivation and fan it into a real fire.

Parents can do two things to help internally motivate their children. Number one, show interest in them. Showing interest in your teenager and in his projects and activities communicates affirmation and support. One of the worst things parents can do to their teen is ignore him. Teenagers scream for their parents' attention and will eventually get it, one way or another. So when you see him focus his efforts on positive projects or activities, give him your attention. By noticing and affirming him, you will help motivate him to do more.

The second way to internally motivate your teen is to be a personal example to him. When your teenager sees areas of motivation in your life, he will pick up on that interest. It will help him to become passionate about and interested in his own goals. One of the greatest lessons I ever learned was from my father's example. He never *felt* his way into *action*. He always *acted* his way into *feeling*. The most powerful lessons we teach our children are taught by example and not by instruction alone.

Affirmation: *Thank You, Father, that my teen is internally motivated to achieve his goals and fulfill his divine destiny. He focuses his attention on activities and projects related to fulfilling that destiny. As his parent, I provide a motivated and disciplined example and encourage him to reach out for all that God has for him.*

Affirmation Scriptures:
1 Timothy 4:15; Proverbs 13:4; Proverbs 2:1–6;
and Philippians 3:14.

30

Finding the Good Things in Life

I'VE BEEN AROUND optimists, and I've been around pessimists, and I can tell you this: Optimists are a whole lot happier than pessimists. When you look in the Word of God, you see that Jesus was the greatest optimist who ever walked the face of the earth. Jesus chose twelve people to help Him, and together that small group of people utterly changed the world. The twelve disciples He picked were totally human and definitely not divine. The men on His staff had tainted backgrounds, illiteracy problems, and seasons of walking in fear and cowardice. But He believed in those twelve, and ultimately they helped Him change the world.

Paul the Apostle was another great leader who continually looked on the bright side. While still in prison, he wrote to the Philippians that he wanted everyone to know his imprisonment had helped spread the gospel (Phil. 1:12, 14). Now, it takes an optimist to say something like that. He went on to say that because of his imprisonment, many Christians had gained confidence and become much bolder in telling others about Christ. This statement came from a man who, because of his imprisonment, could no longer preach publicly or have free access to people. Yet he said that being imprisoned had helped him to spread the gospel. It made other Christians bolder in their witness. His optimistic outlook enabled him to make such bold statements.

Some time ago, I read an article about some psychologists studying a set of twins. One twin was an extreme optimist, whereas the other twin was a full-blown pessimist. They took the pessimistic twin and tried to create the most euphoric situation possible for him—they purchased hundreds of dollars' worth of toys and put the little kid in the room with a closed-circuit television. Telling him he would be in there for a while, they said he could play with anything he wanted. Within a few minutes the child was sitting in the middle of the floor crying. When the psychologists came in, they asked him what was wrong. He said there were too many toys and that he might break one. Now, that's a pessimist!

Then they took the optimistic child and created the most appalling environment they could. They loaded up a room with a foot of horse manure and told the little guy they were going to leave him in there for several minutes. Within a few moments the closed-circuit television had zoomed in on him. Immediately, they noticed he was picking up the manure and throwing it around the room, all the while grinning and squealing. Amazed, the psychologists rushed in and asked him, "What are you doing? What are you so happy about?" The little kid looked up and said, "With all this horse manure, I know there has to be a pony under here somewhere." That is a true optimist, always looking for the pony under the manure. When it comes to your teenager, you should be positive too. No matter how many dumb things they do, you need to realize that God still believes in them and so should you.

My own life was turned around by an optimistic little grandmother. Even though I had been kicked out of three schools for drug and alcohol use, she kept telling me that some day I was going to be all that God had called me to be. I could never get away from those words. When you see your teenager as a success and not a failure, a blessing and not a curse, a human and not an alien, it will reinforce a positive self-image. Choosing to be optimistic in your outlook will affect not only you, it will affect the lives of the people around you as well.

Affirmation: *Father, I thank You that my teen is a Holy Ghost–filled, non-compromising, sold-out child of God. She loves You with all her heart and pursues Your calling on her life with intelligence and dedication. A blessing to all those around her, she is surrounded by favor and success.*

Affirmation Scriptures:

Philippians 3:12; 2 Corinthians 9:8; and Proverbs 4:18.

31

Laugh at Yourself

ONE OF THE MOST common mistakes parents make is to take themselves too seriously. We have all made mistakes in parenting and will continue to make more during our lifetimes, but we are improving. I'm a better parent this year than I was last year, and I will be a better parent next year than I am this year. It is important to realize that we are not perfect parents. There is only one perfect parent, and that is our heavenly Father. It is equally important to recognize there is only one perfect child, and His name is Jesus! The key is that when we fall down we need to be quick to get back up. It's better to jump back up and get going again than to lie down and wallow in guilt and condemnation: "For a righteous man may fall seven times / And rise again" (Prov. 24:16 NKJV).

Several years ago during the Christmas holidays, my son was learning to walk. We were at his grandparents' house, and everyone was there. When they noticed my boy attempting to turn loose of the couch and walk several feet over to the table, they all started cheering him on. You would have thought it was Super Bowl Sunday and our team was running the football down the field for a touchdown on the opening kickoff. But after two wobbly steps, he fell down on the thick shag carpet. Do you think everybody just hung their heads, turned away, and said, "It's a shame. He tried to walk, but he fell. I guess he'll never walk again"? No, everybody jumped to their feet and started cheering him on to try it again. After several tries (and our family screaming themselves hoarse for the holidays), he finally made it to the table all by himself that night.

If you have goofed up as a parent, repent and jump back up. You do not have to do penance, crawl across glass, walk on coals of fire, or even wear sackcloth and ashes. Remember that God is producing change in you. Ask forgiveness from those involved and watch what God will do as you climb out of condemnation and move back into His blessings. Don't feel guilty about *not* feeling guilty. Most of the time, it's much easier to forgive others than it is to forgive yourself. Forgiving yourself after you mess up can be extremely difficult. The accuser of the brethren will be screaming into your ear, "You really messed up now. There's no coming back from this one." Realize that, as you repent and put your shortcomings under the blood, Jesus paid the price for your failures. Then you can pick up with a fresh start and go at it again. And laugh at yourself. It'll do you good and will help you shake off all the condemnation. The enemy hates joy and is a master at robbing you of laughter.

The other day I was quite testy with my son as I was trying to catch a flight to go speak. I just couldn't seem to zip up the suitcase I had packed for the trip. I was already ten minutes late in leaving to catch my flight when the phone rang. Then I heard the doorbell. To make it even worse, I couldn't find my keys, and my son was following me from room to room saying, "Dad . . . Dad . . . Dad." Finally, I snapped at him, "Not now!" But he just stood between me and the door I was trying to answer. I asked him to move out of the way so I could get to the door. After signing for the FedEx package that had arrived, I turned and looked at my son standing there. Feeling guilty and frustrated, I asked, "Tell me. What is it, son?"

"I just wanted to say, have a great trip," he said with a crooked smile.

Time stopped. Realizing my pitiful attitude, I burst out laughing. Suddenly my priorities changed. Neither the phone nor the FedEx person nor the flight mattered nearly as much as my son. Shaking my head, I looked him in the eyes and said, "I'm sorry for snapping at you." Then we hugged, and I told him I loved him.

So, take a lesson from me. Quit wallowing in condemnation and self-pity and stop taking yourself so seriously. Go ahead and laugh at yourself occasionally—it will do your life good.

Affirmation: *Father, I thank You that the joy of the Lord is my strength. You are still working on me because You promise to complete the work You began in me. When I fall, I thank You that I get back up. You are quick to forgive and restore my life from destruction. I have made up my mind not to let the enemy steal my joy, because Jesus said that His joy will remain in me and that my joy will be full.*

Affirmation Scriptures:
Nehemiah 8:10; Philippians 2:13; Philippians 1:6; Proverbs 24:16; Psalm 86:5; Psalm 103:4–5; and John 15:11.

32

Affirming Your Teenager

IT IS TRUE that your words carry power. The things you say to your teen will either give life or produce death. As a parent, God has given you spiritual jurisdiction over your teenager. The way to release His power in your child's life is through your words: "Death and life are in the power of the tongue, / And those who love it will eat its fruit" (Prov. 18:21 NKJV).

We're all going to eat some type of fruit. But it's up to us what kind of fruit it will be. We're the ones who will determine whether it will be good fruit or bad fruit. We have the ability to surround our teenager, our spouse, and our business either with life or death. What you say *about* your teenager is as important as what you say *to* your teenager. Do not deceive yourself into thinking, *It's okay. She never actually heard me say that negative thing about her, so it won't hurt her.* According to the Bible, it doesn't matter whether you say it in front of her or behind her back, your words still produce either life or death.

A father once came up to me and began to talk about what a loser his son was. "He's never going to make it," he said, shaking his head and scowling. I knew the son and was quite surprised to hear him say that type of thing about his boy. Sure, the kid wasn't perfect, but who is? All I had ever noticed about his son was his incredible potential. My expression must have reflected my surprise, because the father was quick to add, "Oh, I never tell my son this." Even though he may have never told his son he was a loser, he had still surrounded him with negative words. Eventually that dad will say something destructive in front of his teenager because negative thoughts have filled his heart.

Jesus had a lot to say about words:

You will have whatever you say. (see Mark 11:23)

We will give an account for every idle word that we speak. (see Matt. 12:36)

Our mouths speak out of the abundance of our hearts. (see Matt. 12:34)

We can draw good treasures out of our heart with our words. (see Luke 6:45)

If you have found yourself having a "mouth" problem, I have something to tell you. It's not a mouth problem. It's a heart problem. The good news is, you can change. God is in the heart-changing business. He has given us some simple instructions in Joshua 1:8:

This Book of the Law shall not depart from your mouth, but you shall meditate in it day and night, that you may observe to do according to all that is written in it. For then you will make your way prosperous, and then you will have good success. (NKJV)

Pray God's Word over your teenager. Don't let His words depart from your mouth. Agree with what God says about your teenager and declare, "She is blessed of the Lord and will do great exploits. God has big plans for her life, plans to prosper her and give her a hope and a future!" You can boldly proclaim this promise over your teen because it comes right out of Scripture (see Jer. 29:11 and Dan. 11:32). This promise belongs to her personally.

Meditate on the good. The enemy will try to paint the worst picture possible by turning a molehill into a mountain. If you meditate on the negative long enough, it will get into your heart. Whatever gets into your heart will come out of your mouth at some point. It is just that simple. Meditating on God's promises will get His Word into your heart, eventually causing it to come out of your mouth with change-producing power!

Do what the Book says—*declare* God's Word. *Meditate* on God's Word. And then *do* God's Word. Remember that it is the doer of the Word who will be blessed in all his deeds. If we want to get results, we must do what the Word says: "If you want a happy life and good days, / keep your tongue from speaking evil, / and keep your lips from telling lies. / Turn away from evil and do good. / Work hard at living in peace with others" (1 Peter 3:10–11 NLT).

Positive results come from doing good, not just hearing or thinking positive thoughts. So act on God's Word. It will affect your heart, which will affect your words, which will affect everything around you, including your family and teenagers.

Affirmation: *Heavenly Father, I confess that Your Word is working mightily in me and is producing results. I speak life over my family and over my teenager. No evil will overtake them because I release Your power with the words of my mouth. You are setting a guard over my mouth and keeping watch over my lips to ensure that my words and meditations are pleasing unto You.*

Affirmation Scriptures:
1 Thessalonians 2:13; Psalm 91:10; Proverbs 18:21; Psalm 141:3; and Psalm 19:14.

33

God's Covenant for Your Children

WEBSTER'S DICTIONARY defines the word *covenant* as a formal, binding agreement. Because we have a covenant with almighty God, we do not merely have hope that everything will turn out okay with our teenagers. We have assurance of it. When we receive Jesus as our Lord, God forms a binding agreement with us concerning our children. For this covenant to be activated, however, we must first know what it says, and then we must believe it.

When I bought my last car, I was automatically enrolled as a member of an automobile club. I was so excited about my new car that I really didn't pay much attention to the details of my member benefits. Several months after buying my car, I left my lights on and my battery died. It took me about three hours to find someone with jumper cables to get my car running again. While the kind man was giving me a jump, he said, "It's a shame you're not a member of an auto club. They come out and do this for you. They include it as part of their membership services." I looked at him, shook my head, and said, "I am a member, but I didn't know they would help me." I learned something that day. I have special privileges by being a member of the automobile club. Now, whenever my battery is dead or I lock my keys in my car or even if I run out of gas, I call my auto club. Within minutes they take care of the problem and get me up and running again.

As a child of God, you have a covenant with God that is loaded with benefits. All you have to do is read the "Policy Manual" to find out what those benefits are so you can take advantage of them. The enemy would love to steal, kill, and destroy your family and the lives of your teenagers, but you can put a stop to it. Your family does not have to be ruined by a lack of knowledge (Hos. 4:6). God has made a powerful covenant with you concerning your children, but it's your responsibility to discover what belongs to you. Once you know the details of your covenant, you must believe that its benefits are yours.

I was talking to a couple who expressed concern because their daughter was drinking and running around with the wrong crowd in college. Having brought her up in church, they felt they had taught her better than that. I smiled and told them, "I have some good news for you." I opened up my Bible to Jeremiah 31:16–17 and had them read it out to me: "But now the LORD says, 'Do not weep any longer, for I will reward you. Your children will come back to you from the distant land of the enemy. There is hope for your future,' says the LORD. 'Your children will come again to their own land'" (NLT).

They looked at me and said, "That's nice, but what does that have to do with us?" I had them open up their Bibles to that passage again. This time I noticed the mother had highlighted the verse in her Bible. She knew about the promise but didn't really believe it applied to her family.

I wish you could have seen that couple light up. Radiant with faith, they said, "So you mean that Scripture in Jeremiah belongs to us and our family?" I replied, "You bet it does. You've got a covenant with God!"

Several months later I received the nicest letter from that couple telling me the story of their daughter's return to faith. They had begun standing on that Scripture and thanking God by faith that their daughter was coming back to the Lord. Within three weeks their daughter called them and asked permission to come home from school. She confessed to her parents that she had been drinking and hanging out with the wrong group of people. Recognizing that God had a future for her, she wanted to change colleges and clean up her life. Her parents welcomed her home and enrolled her in a Christian university. She made new friends, cleaned up her act, and started pursuing her God-given destiny.

God tells us, "For no matter how many promises God has made, they are 'Yes' in Christ. And so through him the 'Amen' is spoken by us to the glory of God" (2 Cor. 1:20 NIV). Every promise from Genesis to Revelation belongs to us. They are all yes, not maybe. The Lord is simply looking for someone to say "amen" or "so be it" to those promises.

It's not enough just to know that God has a covenant with you. You must believe it. In today's world, it takes the supernatural power of God to raise heaven-bound kids in a hell-bent world. And that's exactly what God has given us—His supernatural power.

Affirmation: *Lord, I have been made a partaker of Your covenant of promise because of what Jesus did for me. Every promise You have made in Your Word belongs to me, including promises of peace and prosperity, healing and forgiveness. You have a great future for my family and me. I study Your Word to show myself approved, believing and standing on Your promises for my family and me.*

Affirmation Scriptures:
Ephesians 2:12–13; 2 Corinthians 1:20; Jeremiah 29:11; Psalm 103:3; 2 Timothy 2:15; and Ephesians 6:13.

34

Praying with Your Teenager: The Importance of the Family Altar

WE ALL KNOW that having a personal daily devotional is extremely important. But it's also important to hold devotions with your family on a regular basis. Finding a time for a family altar and devotions can be a challenge. Whether that time is right before bed or first thing in the morning, it needs to be a time when the family can get together and read some Scriptures. The most opportune time to have a family altar may be in the morning, around the breakfast table. Or it might work best to hold devotions in the evening, right before bed when everyone is at home. Some families like to have them around the supper table. Because each family is unique, the best time for family devotions will vary.

Family devotions should be kept short and upbeat the majority of the time. If they become dragged out and heavy, the family will start dreading them. You might try reading a short devotional from a book or take one Scripture and talk about it for a few minutes. Include a practical life application involving something you went through that day or week.

Family members can take turns leading the devotional unless everyone is more comfortable with one person doing it. I have found it works better in our family to take turns. This guarantees the participation of every member of the family at least once during the week.

Because of today's hectic schedules, it's not always practical to hold an official family devotional every single day. Sometimes it's difficult enough just to get everybody to sit down and eat a meal together. Between basketball, church functions, school, traveling, and extracurricular activities, it's practically impossible at our house to sit down and read the Word together at a regularly scheduled time. Of course, it would be ideal to have an official family altar each day, but sometimes we have to settle for an unofficial family devotional time.

Your consistency and lifestyle preach louder than any sermon you could possibly give your teenager. In fact, your lifestyle as a parent preaches a sermon to her on a daily basis. Deuteronomy 11:18–21 says,

> Commit yourselves completely to these words of mine. Tie them to your hands as a reminder, and wear them on your forehead. Teach them to your children. Talk about them when you are at home and when you are away on a journey, when you are lying down and when you are getting up again. Write them on the doorposts of your house and on your gates, so that as long as the sky remains above the earth, you and your children may flourish. (NLT)

Family devotions are important, but don't feel condemnation if you aren't able to have a family altar every single day. Some of the greatest lessons your teenagers will ever learn are experienced through observing you and your lifestyle and attitudes. Through your example, you can teach biblical principles to your teenager at any time—when he is at home, away on a journey, lying down in bed, or getting up in the morning.

After he became a Christian, my father taught me a very important lesson through his example. We were driving along when a car suddenly pulled out in front of us, and he had to slam on the brakes. I was waiting for my dad to begin his normal dialogue (spouting off certain "choice" words) with the other car. But my dad just smiled and shook his head. His behavior puzzled me because it was contrary to what he usually did. I said to him, "Dad, aren't you upset?" He just shook his head at me and said, "I'm not going to let that person steal my joy because the joy of the Lord is my strength." To this day, I have never forgotten that lesson.

As a youth pastor for many years, I experienced preaching by example over and over again. I can tell you with certainty that our teenagers learned more from me out on the basketball court, in fast-food restaurants, and while driving the church van than they ever did from the many sermons I preached. I remember one time in particular when I was with a young man named "Jeff." Jeff and I had just walked into a convenience store. As I went to pay for the gas I had put in the church van, I saw the woman behind the counter. It was apparent she had been crying. I looked at her and said, "Has anybody let you know today that Jesus really loves you?" Well, Jeff freaked out and took off running. He literally dived into the van. As nobody else was in the store, I witnessed to that woman for the next few minutes and found out she was going through a very difficult time in her life. After asking Christ to come into her heart, her whole countenance changed.

When I got into the van with Jeff, he said, "Don't ever do that again!" I asked, "Don't do what again?"

"Witness to people like that," he replied. "Did you see how embarrassed that lady got?"

I responded, "Jeff, you got more embarrassed than that lady did. In fact, I prayed with her, and she received Christ."

I had to take Jeff into the store and show him that the woman had received the Lord. She was radiant with the love of God, a complete contradiction of what she had been just a few minutes before. Jeff never said anything, but I could tell that it had a huge impact on his life.

Several months later we stopped by that same convenience store again. I handed Jeff some cash to pay for the gas I had just purchased. Right after he walked into the store, a group of motorcycle ruffians drove up. These guys looked as if they were ready for a fight. As Jeff's youth pastor, I felt responsible for him, so I prayed, "God, protect Jeff, and if he doesn't come out in three minutes, I'm going in after him."

Well, about fifteen minutes later I decided I needed to go in and save Jeff. But when I opened up the door, I could not believe what I saw. He had all thirteen motorcyclists lined up against the beer cooler and was preaching Jesus Christ to them. Before we left that convenience store, two of them prayed and asked Christ to come into their hearts. When we got back into the church van, I looked at Jeff and said, "What inspired you to do that?" He replied, "When you spoke to the lady several months ago in the convenience store about Jesus, that did something to me on the inside."

So remember, it is our job as parents to talk to our children at all times about God's Word and His biblical principles. We are to talk about them when we are at home and when we are away on a journey, when we are lying down, and when we are getting up. Our lifestyles and attitudes teach our teenagers practical ways to apply God's Word to their lives, preaching the most memorable sermons they will ever hear.

Affirmation: *We make it our goal as a family to spend time together in Your Word every day. Thank You, Father, that our family devotions are a time of joy, fellowship, and instruction in Your Word. I teach the Word to my children at all times, both through my words and my example.*

Affirmation Scriptures:
Deuteronomy 11:18–21; Psalm 5:12; and 1 Timothy 4:12.

35

Attitude:
Dealing with a Smart Mouth

NOTHING LOOKS so bad on a teenager as a smart mouth. In fact, a smart mouth looks bad on anyone. Of course, I'm not referring to an area of intelligence on your body. I mean a mouth that stings, burns, and hurts with the words that come out of it.

Two basic things can cause a teenager to act like a smart aleck. Number one, she may be dealing with insecurity. Or number two, she may be confused. At this age, kids are generally trying to find out about themselves, to discover who they really are. We know that such behavior does not help them find themselves, but kids don't always realize that fact. Often they will test their parents and other adults by seeking out their independence or by trying to show their intelligence and maturity in a perverse manner. They may do this by exhibiting a superior attitude or a false sense of confidence that can be interpreted as cockiness. Either way, this attitude doesn't look or sound good on your teenager.

Some people think that every teenager goes through a smart-mouth period at some point in her life. But that's not true. In fact, under the old covenant, Exodus 21:17 says, "And he who curses his father or his mother shall surely be put to death" (NKJV). The word *curse* in Hebrew means to make light of or to belittle.[1] Disrespect for one's parents was not tolerated under old covenant law. There are many parents who would like to reinstate this law, but I'm grateful (and so are teenagers!) that we are living under a new covenant.

Parents can do a number of things to help prevent their teenager from becoming a smart aleck or, if she already has a problem, to cure her of a disrespectful attitude. First, you need to set her a good example. It is also important to speak the Word over her. In addition, let her know how it makes other people feel when she uses cutting words. You can also help her become secure in the person God made her.

Before trying to help your teenager, you need to make sure you are not the source of the problem. Check to see if you have a smart mouth yourself. We can try to correct our teenagers, but if we're cynical and have a sharp tongue, we must recognize that the problem lies first in us.

First Timothy 4:12 says, "Be an example to the believers in word, in conduct, in love, in spirit, in faith, in purity" (NKJV). The first thing this Scripture mentions is that we are to be examples to believers—including our children—by our words and conduct. If our children have a problem with their words, they may have gotten it from us. If you discover you have a critical or abrasive tongue, stop right now and repent. Then you'll be able to help your teenager overcome her problem.

Once you have taken care of your own mouth, you can speak the Word over your teenager. In the book of Mark, Jesus told us that we are to speak *to* the mountain (Mark 11:23). Most of the time, however, we are great at speaking *about* the mountain. We complain *about* our kids to our friends, and we complain *about* our kids to their teachers and neighbors. But God doesn't say "Speak *about* the mountain." He says, "Speak *to* the mountain"! Declaring God's Word over your child can really move that mountain of cynicism and negative words. Declare Psalm 19:14 over your child, that the words of her mouth and the meditations of her heart are acceptable in the sight of the Lord. Then you can say that your child continually offers up a sacrifice of praise to God in the fruit of her lips that continually give thanks to His name (Heb. 13:15).

Next, proclaim, "No corrupt communication proceeds out of my child's mouth, only what is good for necessary edification, that it imparts grace to all the hearers" (see Eph. 4:29 NKJV). Someone might ask, "What good does that do?" The reason that it works is because you are speaking God's Word. The Bible says that God's Word "shall not return to Me void, / But it shall accomplish what I please, / And it shall prosper in the thing for which I sent it" (Isa. 55:11 NKJV). When you declare God's Word over your teenager, you are releasing the very power of God. And it takes the power of God to tame the tongue!

The third thing you can do to help your teenager stop using cutting words is to tell her how it makes people feel. She may be talking like that and, in all honesty, not even realize the effect it has on people. You are letting her know that talking like that makes people feel put down and ridiculed. Make sure that you also tell her you love her very much and that you know she loves you. Let her know that your relationship with her is too important to be based on disrespect and criticism. Help her find a better way to express herself to you. Sharing this with your teen from a heart of compassion will help you quickly discover the root cause of her smart mouth.

Finally, help her be secure in who she is as a person. Parents can help build security in their teens through four basic methods: affirming the positive in them, praising their personality traits, giving them responsibility, and taking pride in their accomplishments.

First, you need to affirm your child. Find positive things to say about her and about her character. You may need to look around a little bit, but you can always find something positive to say about your child. Once you find something encouraging, say it.

Next, you need to praise her. Let her know that she lights up the room with her smile, that her life blesses other people because of her love for them. Maybe she always stands up for the underdog. As you praise her with sincerity rather than flattery, you will build confidence and security in her.

It is also important to give her responsibility. Now I know this may sound strange to you, but giving her responsibility lets her know that she is important. It also sends a message to her that she does belong to and is an intricate part of the family. She may not like scrubbing the toilets on Wednesday, but she knows it's her job and that the rest of the family depends on her to do it. She realizes that it is her responsibility. Kids will take responsibility if you will give it to them.

Take pride in her achievements. When she does something good, let your friends know, "Hey, that's my girl!" Get excited when she hits a home run or gets onto first base. If she does great academically or shoots an extra point from the free-throw line, go ahead—stand up and shout! She may hang her head and tell you it embarrasses her, but I can promise you this—she is excited that you are taking pride in her achievements. Everyone wants to be around people who use their words to build others up rather than tear them down. Learning the importance of using words that edify others will be one of the greatest lessons your teens will ever learn, one that will last them the rest of their lives.

Affirmation: *Our teen speaks words of respect and edification to those around her. She is secure in knowing who she is in Christ Jesus. We thank You, Father, that we present a good example to her in the words we speak. The words of her mouth and the meditations of her heart are pleasing in Your sight.*

Affirmation Scriptures:
Hebrews 13:15; Philippians 2:13; Ephesians 4:29; and Psalm 19:14.

36

Dealing with Your Anger as a Parent

ANGER IS AN EMOTION that we all experience at one time or another. It's also an emotion we must learn to deal with because it will eventually destroy us if left unchecked. If we fail to control our anger, it will control us. I am sure you are familiar with Ephesians 4:26: "Be angry, and yet do not sin; do not let the sun go down on your anger" (NASB). The *New Living Translation* puts it this way: "'Don't sin by letting anger gain control over you.' Don't let the sun go down while you are still angry." No matter what circumstances give rise to anger, we need to recognize that the anger is our own problem. It's not the problem of the person who made us angry. Nobody can make us do anything. When the Bible says not to let the sun go down on our anger, it is not referring to the other person's anger; it is commanding each of us to deal with our own.

There are so many benefits to gaining control over the emotion called *anger*. Proverbs 16:32 says, "He who is slow to anger is better than the mighty, / And he who rules his spirit than he who takes a city" (NKJV). Your gifts and hard work may help you achieve great things, but it's your character that will keep you there. Many people have achieved success only to lose it all instantly through an outburst of anger or rage. I don't know about you, but I don't want to lose the blessings God has for me, and I surely don't want my teenagers to lose them, either.

God gives us a great word in Proverbs 19:11: "People with good sense restrain their anger; they earn esteem by overlooking wrongs" (NLT). One of the best ways to restrain your anger is to make a decision to overlook any wrongs committed against you. Your teenagers will pick up on your patient attitude and learn from your example, the greatest teacher of all. Often the goal of an angry person, whether conscious or subconscious, is to stir up dissension: "A hothead starts fights; a cool-tempered person tries to stop them" (Prov. 15:18 NLT).

Many times folks get angry in order to gain control, i.e., to intimidate others. If an angry person learns that he can get his own way by yelling and screaming or destroying personal property, he will continue to blow up. But the cool-tempered person realizes he can be strong without becoming irate.

Anger can also be a learned behavior. When you hang around people who are given to anger, you can also become angry. In fact, the Bible warns us in Proverbs 22:24–25 to "make no friendship with an angry man, / And with a furious man do not go, / Lest you learn his ways / And set a snare for your soul" (NKJV). God teaches us not to associate with or hang around people who are prone to anger.

Now sometimes you can't avoid it. Let's say that you're married to a person given to outbursts of anger or you work with someone who loses his temper a lot. Maybe it's a schoolmate or friend of your teen. In these types of situations, you can pray that God will use you to influence them rather than allowing them to influence you.

We can do a number of things to overcome anger in our lives and to help our teenagers overcome anger as well. The first one is confession of our sin to God and prayer. The Bible says, "If we confess our sins, He is faithful and just to forgive us our sins and to cleanse us from all unrighteousness" (1 John 1:9 NKJV). Thank God for fresh starts! Not only does He forgive us, but He also cleanses us. This requires us to confess our sin and not to cover it up.

Next, you need to go to the person with whom you blew up and ask for his forgiveness. James 4:10 says, "Humble yourselves in the sight of the Lord, and He will lift you up"(NKJV). When you go to him and ask for forgiveness, you are actually humbling yourself. God sees this, and He honors it. Doing this will also increase your desire to change because you won't want to keep asking people for their forgiveness for the same thing over and over again. This will stir up in you a real desire for transformation, a desire to overcome your problem with anger.

Third, you need to guard your meditations. Philippians 4:8 says,

> Finally, brethren, whatever things are true, whatever things are noble, whatever things are just, whatever things are pure, whatever things are lovely, whatever things are of good report, if there is any virtue and if there is anything praiseworthy—meditate on these things. (NKJV)

God provides us with specific instructions on the nature of our meditations. Our thoughts need to focus on the positive rather than on the negative. If you continually meditate on negative things, it will begin a slow burn in your attitude. That burn will become a flame and eventually cause an explosion. But if you meditate on the good report, it will keep your mind focused on the positive and off of the negative. The great thing is, you will find yourself enjoying life a whole lot more!

The fourth thing you can do to overcome anger and prevent its outbursts is found in James 5:16: "Confess your trespasses to one another, and pray for one another, that you may be healed. The effective, fervent prayer of a righteous man avails much" (NKJV). There is something about confessing your trespasses, sins, and weaknesses to someone else that helps keep you accountable. Make sure that your accountability person is someone of the same sex (unless it's your spouse). Ask this person to hold you accountable for your emotions and for any outbursts of anger.

These four keys are great for people who realize they have a problem with anger and who desire to change. But if you're dealing with a person who doesn't realize he has a problem (such as your teen), it's best to get him to talk about it first. This, combined with wisdom on your

37

Help! My Teenager Is Angry!

TEEN VIOLENCE has seen a huge increase during the past decade. We see this trend reflected in the greater number of school shootings. Many teens appear to have a considerable amount of rage hidden just below the surface. Like an active volcano, this rage has the potential to explode at any given moment into a fury of words and destructive behavior.

Although many teenagers will experience anger and frustration at various points during their adolescent years, few will exhibit the type of violent behavior described above. Instead of going on a shooting spree, the average teen may give expression to his anger by blowing up at a simple request like washing the dishes or taking out the trash.

The amazing thing is that a tangible reason for your teen's anger often does not even appear to exist. But before you allow yourself to get caught up in his frustration and let it affect you, I encourage you to stop and try to be part of the solution. Ask yourself how you as a parent can best help your child get a grip on his anger and deal with his rage before it has the chance to explode.

A number of things can contribute to the anger experienced by teens while growing up. According to Christian psychologist Dr. James Dobson, one of the reasons that teens get angry is that most teenagers feel frustrated because they are at an in-between stage of their lives:

parents' love for them. I know this may sound somewhat warped, but many teens think like this: *If you really love me, you will be sweet and nice to me even though I am not nice to you.* They are deliberately pushing the envelope in order to test your love. They conclude that if you overreact or become harsh with them because of the way they act, you must not really love them. I know this is a distorted way of thinking, but remember some of the bizarre reasoning you had when you were a teenager!

Do not allow your teenager to manipulate or deceive you into thinking that you are the cause for her outbursts of rage. Remember that we are all responsible for our own actions, regardless of how others treat us. Your teenager can't make you act or react in a certain way. Likewise, you can't make your teen act a certain way either. We all have our own free will.

Although many parents may feel helpless to prevent angry outbursts by their teenagers, parents are able to do certain things to keep their teens' anger in check and prevent it from exploding into an eruption of violence. The following strategies will help parents reinforce discipline and cultivate an understanding of the consequences to negative actions.

Help your teenager to identify that a problem exists. "Houston, we have a problem"—those words echoed through space decades ago, enabling Mission Control to begin fixing the problem *Apollo 13* was encountering and ultimately save the lives of all the astronauts on board. But before Mission Control was able to help them, the crew of *Apollo 13* had to recognize that a problem existed. Helping your teen realize that she even has a problem can be an incredible breakthrough. To be effective, you need to do this in an attitude of love and with a desire to help rather than a desire to condemn. If your motives are retaliatory or defensive in nature, your teen will see it and will probably dig her heels in even deeper.

Although she may not be able to receive correction from you right away, if you share with her out of a spirit of loving concern, it will cause her to think more about what you said. Eventually, your caring attitude will allow your words to sink in and impact her actions.

Encourage her to see the big picture. Help her to look down the road and visualize how her angry outbursts could affect her future. Encourage her to ask herself these questions before flying off the handle: "What are some of the results of being angry and giving vent to negative feelings? Can I avoid an angry outburst if I stop to think about the consequences before I light the fuse?" Looking at the big picture can help your teen to look past the feelings she is experiencing in the moment and help her to assess the real effect of giving unrestrained vent to them.

Ask God to give her a revelation of His love and peace. When you ask God to move on her behalf, you are giving permission to His Holy Spirit to do a work in your teen that will not happen without your invitation. God will never move in where He is not invited.

God gave Adam dominion over the earth, and man gave that dominion to Satan when he fell from grace. That is when Satan became the god of this world. Because God will not go beyond His own jurisdiction, we must invite Him in if we want His help. We must give Him the dominion over our lives. That is why we must ask. In Matthew 6:8, the Word tells us that our Father in heaven knows what we need before we ask Him. Notwithstanding, Jesus went on to tell us in Matthew 7:7 that we still need to ask God for what we want. Then, after we ask God, He will give it to us. I am convinced that one of the reasons God does not intervene more in our teenagers' lives is that we do not invite Him to do so.

Monitor your teen's use of the various media forms. If your child likes to listen to violent or sexual lyrics in music or play violent video games, her thinking will probably be affected. The same with movies and TV—the more aggressive the shows, the more negative the impact on her behavior. Remember the old adage "garbage in, garbage out." Recognizing the influence of our thoughts on our actions, the Bible tells us to meditate on that which is good, kind, and lovely (see

Phil. 4:8). The Word also tells us that we are not to be conformed to this world, but rather to be transformed by the renewing of our minds (see Rom. 12:2). Regular exposure to violent musical lyrics, video games, movies, or television shows has just the opposite effect of renewing our minds; it will cause us to adopt the ways of the world rather than be transformed.

Encourage your child to talk out her anger. If you allow her to talk to you about her frustrations and feelings, they will not resurface in the form of undesirable, aggressive behavior later down the road. I personally have noticed that teens who express their anger verbally are less likely to express it behaviorally. Think of it as a safety valve—giving vent to pressure to prevent an explosion. It may also help her to realize that her anger is unjustified and cause her to change the way she feels.

Declare your love for your child. After the storm has passed, it is important that you verbalize your love for her. Reaffirm that you want the best for her. By doing this, you will communicate that you are disagreeing with her behavior and not attacking her personally.

Hug your teen. Physical affection can go a long way toward communicating love and acceptance for your teenager. Sometimes all it takes is a little pat on the back or a touch of the hand to say, "I think you're a great kid, and I love you." Nonverbal expressions of love can "soothe the savage beast." It can ward off an angry outburst before it has the chance to get started. Many parents draw back from showing physical affection for their child once she hits adolescence, but the truth is that children never stop needing a parent's love or the physical expression of that love.

Don't provoke your teen to wrath. God's Word commands parents not to provoke their children to wrath, for good reason (Eph. 6:4). As parents, we are acutely aware of what hot buttons to push if we want to get a reaction out of our teenagers. This can cause great discouragement on the part of our children and eventually discourage them to the point of giving up. They may even throw in the towel and quit trying. Believe the best, talk the best, and desire the best for your child, even when she is not behaving the best. Doing this will let her know you're pulling for her and will pay off in your relationship for the rest of your life. Sometimes you may have to exercise tough love; just remember to keep your motives pure. Retaliatory or vengeful motives will only serve to fuel her anger and instill rebellion.

Parents can play a major role in helping their teens deal effectively with anger. Through your loving concern and wisdom, your teenager can successfully confront her negative feelings without giving vent to them in a destructive or negative way. Encourage her to talk out her feelings with you, and listen when she does. Be involved in your child's life; find out what she listens to and what she watches. Most of all, let her know that you love her unconditionally and desire only the best for her life.

Affirmation: *Thank You, Lord, that my teen is not easily angered. She fills her mind with godly and peaceful thoughts and does not dwell on that which is contentious or full of strife. She turns away from violent video games, music, TV shows, and movies. I do not provoke my teen to wrath. Instead, I assure her of my love for her and my desire to see the very best for her.*

Affirmation Scriptures:
Ephesians 6:4; Romans 12:2; Philippians 4:8; and 1 John 3:18–20.

38

Helping Your Teen Get Rid of Her Temper

REMEMBER WHEN your kids were toddlers and first learning to walk? Everything they did was cute. Even when they got angry or pouted, it was hard not to laugh. Their little scrunched-up red faces and temper tantrums were so amusing.

It reminds me of the story a friend once told me about his first birthday party. All of his relatives were there for the celebration of the big mile marker for this one-year-old. While eating his ice cream, he made such a mess of his face that everyone began to giggle. This didn't make him happy, so he put the empty bowl on his head to hide from them. That made the family laugh even harder. Then he began flinging cake in every direction—at the refrigerator, on the carpet, at the family. Any direction his little hands went, the cake also flew. His family doubled over in hysterics. For months after this messy but entertaining episode, his grandmother continued to discover cake crumbs all over her kitchen.

These cute little tantrums quickly turn into a real problem when children become adults. News programs constantly broadcast stories of road rage, teen violence, and school shootings, making it all too clear that tempers are not cute and can have serious consequences when uncontrolled.

But before we panic and try to cast this "Yosemite Sam demon" out of our kids, we need to examine the root of all anger problems: "Now the works of the flesh are evident, which are . . . outbursts of wrath" (Gal. 5:19–20 NKJV). Those controlled by the flesh will experience problems with anger. They are not bad people with permanent character flaws; they are just flesh-ruled. In fact, all of us have areas we need to control. We need to see anger as simply another work of the flesh that we can overcome: "But put on the Lord Jesus Christ, and make no provision for the flesh, to fulfill its lusts" (Rom. 13:14 NKJV).

A lack of discipline in other areas of our lives can increase the hold of the old nature on our attitudes. If we refuse to put limits on our leisure time, food consumption, or television viewing, we will feed our flesh and strengthen its control over us. We need to temper the desires of the flesh and feed the spirit instead. When we fellowship with other believers, pray, or read the Bible, we feed our spirit and make it more difficult for the flesh to rule over us. We give place to the Holy Spirit, who empowers us to tame our tempers and fleshly desires.

Your teenager can do some practical things to alleviate stress when he feels his temper rising. Encourage him to take some deep breaths and count to ten (or a thousand if he has to) before letting his anger boil over. Teach him to pause long enough to get a grip on his feelings and stop a reaction before it gets started.

Train your child to speak only things that are edifying, even in situations of great provocation. There is an old saying: "If you can't say something good, don't say anything at all." Putting this principle into practice will help him avoid losing control and blowing up.

When all else fails, and he is about to lose her cool, encourage your teen to walk away from the situation: "Flee also youthful lusts; but pursue righteousness, faith, love, peace with those who call on the Lord out of a pure heart" (2 Tim. 2:22 NKJV). If he walks away, he will not have the opportunity to blow up at the *object* of his irritation.

Parents can help their children overcome anger by providing a winning environment for them. We need to ensure that the authority figures (especially parents) in their lives exemplify a controlled and godly temperament: "Keep away from angry, short-tempered people, or you will learn to be like them and endanger your soul" (Prov. 22:24–25 NLT). If you lose your temper and yell or throw things, your teen will see your example and emulate it. Many a country song has been written about this kind of behavior. Remember that parents serve as the most important role model their children will ever see. Use your influence to steer your children in the direction of self-control rather than anger.

Be careful how you discuss your child's behavior. Do not use words like "his temper" or "her temper." Phrases like these communicate ownership of the problem by your child. If you constantly connect him to an angry attitude, you will make it more difficult for him to overcome it. You can help your teen by focusing on the positive, pointing toward him progress and ultimate deliverance from this stronghold of the flesh. Doing this will give him the momentum to ultimately succeed, even if he temporarily messes up.

Do everything you can to emphasize his victories rather than his failures. Remind him that the Lord is greater than any problem and can help him to overcome. When we stop pointing fingers at our children and start holding their hands instead, they will begin to believe they can overcome. And once they realize they are overcomers, they will succeed in changing their behavior.

Finally, parents need to ensure that their children do not use anger to get what they want. If we give in to them because they throw a tantrum, we only serve to reinforce the problem. It's hard to convince a teen to stop doing something that helps her get exactly what she wants. Responding to angry outbursts with anything other than discipline reinforces the negative behavior.

While in college, a friend of mine was asked to baby-sit two cute little red-haired boys. He was not chosen to do this job because of his incredible ability to entertain children. In fact, he found out later that he won this privilege by default. No one else would take on the challenge without a set of earplugs, full body armor, and the National Guard on call as backup.

With that in mind, the parents dropped off the two little boys. First, they started screaming because their parents left. Then they pitched a fit because they couldn't eat the food they wanted or go where they desired. After about forty-five minutes of nonstop, high-pitched screaming, they finally settled down and stopped. The sound of quiet was music to my friend's ears. The kids were happy; he was happy. After they finally understood that throwing temper tantrums was not going to help them get their way, they started behaving better.

My friend couldn't wait to show the parents the change in their boys' behavior. But something amazing happened when the parents walked through the doors. The kids started crying and screaming for this, that, and the other thing. And it worked! Through their responses, the parents had trained their kids to use temper tantrums to get whatever they wanted. I don't know about you, but I prefer my cute little red-haired boys without the screaming.

By responding appropriately to our teenagers' angry outbursts, we will show them that anger doesn't help them achieve the desired results. It may take some time to get this message across to them, but they will eventually understand it. It will help them bring their flesh under control and not give place to wrath or anger in their lives.

Affirmation: *I present a godly example of spirit-controlled attitudes and lives to my children. Our children refuse to let anger rule over them and do not give in to outbursts of wrath. They live self-controlled lives and speak only things that are edifying to those around them.*

Affirmation Scriptures:
Romans 13:14; 2 Timothy 2:22; and Ephesians 4:32.

39

Teenagers and Rebellion

IN THE JEWISH CULTURE, there is a ceremony called the *bar mitzvah,* which celebrates the transition from childhood to adulthood. For boys, this celebration occurs on their thirteenth birthday. A similar celebration, the *bat mitzvah,* takes place for girls on their twelfth birthday. From that day forward, the young person is considered fully responsible for his or her own actions. They are perceived as adults, accountable for their own behavior.

In the United States and Western Europe, we call the transition period between the ages of twelve and eighteen *adolescence.* It's a no-man's-land; adolescents are considered to be neither child nor adult. Low expectations and a lack of responsibility often characterize this state of limbo. Its effect can be quite negative, causing parents frustration and irritation with their often-rebellious teenagers. Teens experience a new level of freedom during adolescence that will breed rebellion if not accompanied by increased responsibility.

I really believe the Jewish culture is on the right track with their coming-of-age commemoration. Rabbi Neil Kurshan, assessing the impact of the bar mitzvah and the bat mitzvah on Jewish teens, wrote,

I have often marveled at the transformation which a bar or bat mitzvah can bring about in the life of a thirteen-year-old . . . Contrary to popular impression, the ceremony does not transform a thirteen-year-old into an adult overnight. After the ceremony, a parent still lives with the adolescent who has to be reminded to clean up his or her room, to do his or her homework, and to help around the house. At its best, however, the bar mitzvah demonstrates both to the thirteen-year-old and to all those present that a young person is growing toward adulthood and toward responsibility and obligations to a broader community.[1]

Through working with troubled teenagers over the years, I have noticed that most teens rebel because their parents place frequent and often unbending demands on them. This rigid approach does not allow room for needed growth and development in the adolescent. Child psychiatrist Dr. Grace Ketterman wrote,

If parents refuse to allow their children to grow, a vicious cycle can develop. As parents become more unyielding, the child becomes more guilt-ridden. The more hopeless the child feels, the worse he acts, because he doesn't know how else to express the way he feels inside. And the worse the child acts, the more determined the parents become to make him behave.[2]

The tighter we try to grip our teenagers, the farther away they will move from us. Consider the following scriptural principle not only as it pertains to finances, but also as it applies to raising your teen: "There is one who scatters, yet increases more; / And there is one who withholds more than is right, / But it leads to poverty" (Prov. 11:24 NKJV). When you try to hang on to "more than is right," you will end up losing valuable ground with your child. The key here is to understand what is right. Every child is an individual and develops differently. God will give you supernatural wisdom and grace to help you determine what is right for your child. He knows you need His help. Remember that your child must develop into an adult—she has no other option. To facilitate her proper development, you need to give her room to grow both in her level of responsibility and in her individuality.

If your child has taken a plunge into an attitude and lifestyle of rebellion, there is still hope. I am living proof that God can restore anyone back to his family, no matter how far he may have drifted. My mom affectionately refers to my teenage years as "a mother's worst nightmare." But, at the age of seventeen, Jesus radically changed my life and completely restored my relationship with my family.

The first step to the journey home is to find out the reason for your teen's rebellion. Most of the time you will discover that your teen is not rebelling against you, but rather against some value for which you stand. Continually changing the rules on your teen can be another factor. Doing this can be a real bummer for her. Remember: Consistency is key!

Keep the communication lines open. When these go down, you have nothing else with which to work. Stay sweet, hear your teenager out, and refuse to get offended easily. If you are determined to dominate the conversation and use your parental authority to get your own way, you are setting yourself up for a major power struggle with your teen. Occasionally, you may need a third party to keep the conversation going in the right direction and to prevent getting bogged down with minor details. Family counselors are experts at keeping a conversation focused on the main issues and getting to the core of the problem so it can be resolved.

Remember that you are the parent, and your teenager is the child. Although it may not appear on the outside that your teen wants to get along with you, I can assure you that she does. But it's your responsibility to take the first step. Don't wait for her to take the first step. You do it.

Affirmation: *Thank You, Father, that my children walk in obedience to You and to Your Word. Because Your commands are not burdensome or*

119

overbearing, they find delight in doing Your will. I refuse to take offense easily and make it a priority to keep the communication lines between us open.

Affirmation Scriptures:

Titus 3:1; Proverbs 1:8; Isaiah 1:19–20; and 2 Corinthians 10:5.

40

Body Piercing and Tattoos

IN THE SEARCH for individualism and personal identity, some teens look for identifying marks to make a statement. On the average, I have about one teen a week ask me what I think about body piercing and tattoos. My usual response is "What do your parents think about it?" The Scripture has some interesting things to say on this subject. On the subject of tattoos, God commanded the children of Israel, saying: "You shall not make any cuttings in your flesh for the dead, nor tattoo any marks on you: I am the LORD" (Lev. 19:28 NKJV). Now, before you run off half-cocked in an antitattoo hysteria fit, you need to realize that in the book of Leviticus, God was referring to tattoos related to godless religious ceremonies. Such cuttings were associated with pagan cults that tattooed their followers as a symbol of mourning the dead.[1] So in this particular instance, the marks were a part of pagan worship. This is quite different from today's society where most people get tattoos just because it is trendy. It's not involved in devotion to the dead or demon worship. I am quite certain a butterfly tattoo on your girl's ankle will not keep her out of heaven, and a cross tattooed on your son's arm will not send him to hell. However, if they get tired of a particular tattoo, it is a major job to take it off. As an alternative to a permanent tattoo, consider having them apply and reapply a temporary tattoo (the same one). See if they still like it after a period of two years or after they turn eighteen. In most cases, they'll get tired of it after the first six months.

Most of the time, teens want a tattoo because it seems cool. They may have watched some of their friends get tattoos, so now they want one. Nothing to be alarmed about, parents. Now, if your child begs to get the numbers 666 placed on his right hand or forehead, that is grounds for concern. Check out Revelation 13:16–18:

> He required everyone—great and small, rich and poor, slave and free—to be given a mark on the right hand or on the forehead. And no one could buy or sell anything without that mark, which was either the name of the beast or the number representing his name. Wisdom is needed to understand this. Let the one who has understanding solve the number of the beast, for it is the number of a man. His number is 666. (NLT)

Let us look at body piercing next. When it comes to this subject, the Word has quite a bit to say. In searching the Scriptures, I found that earrings and nose rings were quite popular among men, women, and children in the ancient world (Ex. 32:2–3; Num. 31:50; Judg. 8:25–26; and Ex. 35:22). Not only was it considered quite fashionable by the upper and middle classes, but it was also sometimes used by slaveowners to mark their "bond slaves":

> But suppose your servant says, "I will not leave you," because he loves you and your family, and he is well off with you. In that case, take an awl and push it through his earlobe into the door. After that, he will be your servant for life. You must do the same for your female servants. (Deut. 15:16–17 NLT)

When Abraham told his right-hand man (probably Eliezer) to go to his home country and pick out a wife for his son, the servant asked God to help him find the right woman for Isaac. When he found the woman who met all the qualifications, Abraham's servant had a ring placed in her nose (Gen. 24:47). This act is one of the things that won Rebekah's heart for Isaac.

When considering whether or not to allow your teen to get a tattoo, remember that he will eventually grow up. He only has one chance to make a first impression, so encourage him to make it a good one. People are often affected by social biases against things such as tattoos or the piercing of the body. In my personal opinion, tattoos and body piercing can hinder efforts to build a relationship with someone, minister the gospel, or even close a business deal. Having tattoos up and down your arm, a ring in your nose, or a pierced tongue can definitely limit your effectiveness and narrow the scope of people with whom you can build a relationship. Your teenager can always take out an earring or nose ring, but it will be more difficult for him to cover up a tattoo on the side of his face. Removing a tattoo costs money and can be painful.

Communication is imperative. Give your teen an opportunity to share how he or she feels about this subject and lay it out on the table for discussion. I cannot tell you the number of parents who have freaked out when their high schooler came home with a "cool earring in his eyebrow" or a strange-looking tattoo on his body. If this happens to you, you don't need to disown your child, have him change his last name, or even put him on the next space shuttle to a faraway planet. It will work out!

Affirmation: *My child is not caught up in trends or fads. He is not swayed by the actions of those around him, but instead makes wise and insightful decisions that positively impact his future and ministry. He looks to Christ for his identity and does not look to the approval of those around him to find his security.*

Affirmation Scriptures:
1 Timothy 4:12; Proverbs 4:11; and Ephesians 6:10.

41

Drug and Alcohol Prevention

ONE OF THE NUMBER-ONE reasons teenagers get involved with drugs and alcohol is because they want to be accepted by the people they hang around with. Show me your friends, and I'll show you how you will turn out. As the Word says, "Can two walk together, unless they are agreed?" (Amos 3:3 NKJV).

It's so important to monitor the quality of people with whom your children hang around. You need to instill in them the knowledge and ability to discern between peers who build them up and peers who tear them down. People seem to gravitate toward people who affirm them. If they don't get affirmation at home, they'll get it at school or from their friends. They will find it somewhere, but it's best if it comes from you as their parent.

Every person has a yearning to be accepted by her peers. It's a driving desire, especially during the teen years. These are the years when teens establish their independence and form their own goals and character. One of the greatest lessons we can ever learn is that we will never be able to please everyone. We have to stand up for what we believe is right and draw behavioral parameters that correspond with our morals and convictions. Many times this involves using a two-letter word few people have the guts to use, but one that demands great respect. That word is *no*. Once a teen or an adult begins to use this word, she will also begin to define her character, establish her destiny, and set a course for life.

You may have heard the story about the old man and his grandson who decided to take a trip into town to get supplies. The old man put his grandson on his donkey, named Himmey. As they started on their journey and rounded the first bend, they heard their neighbors talking. "Can you believe that old man walking while that young boy is riding the donkey? If they had any sense, the old man would ride the donkey and make the young boy walk." So the grandfather pulled the boy off the donkey, made him walk, and began riding the donkey himself.

After they had traveled a little farther, they saw some more people and overheard them saying, "Look how silly those people are. They should both be riding that donkey." So the grandfather pulled the boy up on the donkey, and they proceeded on their way.

Right before getting to an old rope bridge, they noticed some people talking to each other. "Can you believe how mean those folks are to that poor donkey? If they were good people, they would carry the donkey." Both riders got off Himmey and began to carry him across the rope bridge. Suddenly the bridge started swinging, and the grandfather and the boy lost their grip. The donkey plunged into the water and swam away, never to be seen again by the grandfather and the boy. The moral of the story is, "If you try to please everyone, you'll lose your Himmey."

How many people do you know who have lost their Himmey because they try to please everyone? Many immoral teens will target your teenager because of her morality. The reason they do this is because of the guilt they themselves feel. They feel that if they can get a good moral person to do the same wrong things they are doing—drinking, smoking, doing drugs, etc.—then it must be okay. They think, *Look, I got this girl to do it, and she goes to church.* People do all sorts of things to appease their guilt, but there is only one thing that can get rid of it. That is the blood of Jesus: "How much more, then, will the blood of Christ . . . cleanse our consciences from acts that lead to death, so that we may serve the living God!" (Heb. 9:14 NIV). There are three keys to helping your teen remain drug and alcohol free in today's society. First, be an example of drug-free living. Parents also need to make their teenagers aware of the destructive properties of drug use. Finally, keep the communication lines open between you and your teenager.

When your teen sees you stand up for what is right and realizes you have the backbone to say no, she will be more apt to do likewise. On the other hand, if she sees you run to alcohol or to a medicine cabinet to cope with the pressures of life, she will learn to do the same. What a great message you preach with your lifestyle when you go through difficult experiences the right way. When your children see you pray, stand on God's Word, and find peace through Him, you preach a message to them through your actions that they will never forget.

Children need to see the negative realities of drug use. Much of the media paints a completely different picture of the effects of drugs and alcohol than what is true. Between the cute beer commercials and the movies depicting drug abuse with virtually no negative results, the media has painted an off-kilter view of them. They fail to show the destroyed lives, the ripped-apart families, and the broken hearts left behind in the wake of this destructive lifestyle.

We need to bring balance to the picture and answer our children's questions, even the embarrassing ones like, "What's wrong with Uncle Bill?" or "Why is Daddy's business friend going through such a hard time with his family?" or "Why did my cousin get put in jail?" Each of these situations presents a powerful lesson in life for your child to remember: People are responsible for their own actions.

Keep the communication lines with your teenager open. Communication takes work, and it starts at an early age. If you have developed a good, healthy relationship with your child, it will make the teen years much easier. But if you have not, it is still not too late to start. When they are faced with tough decisions or pressure from their peers, they'll be more likely to come to you for advice in the middle of those temptations if you have an established strong relationship with them.

By raising your children to be God-pleasers rather than people-pleasers, you will help them develop the backbone needed to say no to peer pressure. Teach them to stand up for what is right, both through your words and by your example. And remember to keep the dialogue going. They need to know they can come to you for wisdom and help, that the lines of communication are always open.

Affirmation: *Thank You that my children choose quality friends, friends who will influence them for good and not for evil. They have no desire to use drugs or alcohol because they know that You, God, are their source of happiness. The communication lines between me and my children are open, and they feel comfortable talking with me about any decisions or situations they may face.*

Affirmation Scriptures:
Romans 12:1–2; John 10:10; 2 Timothy 2:25–26; and James 1:12.

42

Help! I Think My Teen Is on Drugs!

PREVENTION IS GREAT, but sometimes it's not enough. Even after you have done all you know to do—wham!—the problem comes home. You find out your teen is on drugs. Don't panic. You're not in this alone. Hundreds of thousands of people have been through your same situation and have come out victorious. And don't forget that you have a secret weapon—God!

One of the enemy's first lines of attack is to convince us we are in this all by ourselves. He tells us that no one can possibly understand our situation. Let me start out by saying this: That is a lie of the enemy. When the enemy attacks us, God's Word says that we are to "take a firm stand against him, and be strong in your faith. Remember that Christians all over the world are going through the same kind of suffering you are" (1 Peter 5:9 NLT). Did you catch that? Our Christian brothers and sisters all over the world are going through the same kind of suffering we are. It's so good to know that other people have not only gone through the same thing, but they have also come out on the other side in victory!

In addition to finding support from other believers, you will find God working right beside you in the middle of your crisis:

For we are God's fellow workers. (1 Cor. 3:9 NKJV)

We then, as workers together with Him. (2 Cor. 6:1 NKJV)

The Lord working with them and confirming the word through the accompanying signs. (Mark 16:20 NKJV)

God is working with us, and we are working with Him. Let me assure you that no matter how bad it looks, all things are possible to him who believes. *Get ready for your turnaround.* I want you to know that I speak from experience. God turned me around in just thirty seconds. I went from being the school drug dealer and class failure to becoming an honor-roll student elected as senior class president. I was also awarded the first full scholarship at the school for my leadership capabilities and exemplary conduct. Believe me when I say this: All things *are* possible!

Don't disqualify yourself from God performing this same miracle for you and your teen. The good news is that God shows no partiality (see Acts 10:34). That means that if He did it for me, He will also do it for your teen. Through my work helping teens across the nation, I have discovered some keys that will really help to get your teenager over his drug problem and back on track with his God-given destiny.

First, do not live in denial. Maybe you found a vial of white powder or a plastic baggy with pills while cleaning out your teen's pockets. Or you found some funny-looking cigarettes in his chest of drawers. Your first response is to try to convince yourself that it's just a part of his science project. Your brain will come up with all sorts of ideas to convince you this isn't really happening. But don't fool yourself. The evidence is right in front of you. If you see billowing black smoke and fire trucks outside your door, and you hear your smoke detector going off, you can be sure there's a fire in the house. The first step toward getting your answer is to recognize the existence of a problem.

Second, do not shift blame. Blame shifting is actually another form of denial. Blaming others for your child's actions will just prolong his journey back home. You can tell yourself, "This really isn't *Billy's* fault; it's his friends' fault." But when you head down this path, you make it hard to get back on the road to recovery. Although his friends may help reinforce his wrong actions, they are not the cause. They are only a reflection of his problem. The blood of Jesus cleanses us from all sin, not from all excuses (see 1 John 1:9). Once your teen confesses his sin as sin and stops trying to push responsibility for his actions off on someone else, God will be able to move in to forgive and restore.

Third, do not blow up. You may feel disgraced, humiliated, and embarrassed, but don't lose your cool. If you get into a screaming match with your child, it will only serve to polarize him farther away from you. Doing so will isolate him and greatly aggravate the situation.

Next, be balanced. Without jumping to conclusions, face the facts. Don't ignore the problem in hopes that it will go away. And do not give your impression of a nuclear warhead detonating on impact. Without closing your eyes to the situation, discuss it with your teenager. Remember to be slow to speak, slow to anger, and quick to forgive (see James 1:19; Eph. 4:32). This doesn't mean you should be lax in your discipline. But keep in mind that reconciliation is your goal. Try to keep the communication lines open as you seek to find a solution together.

Also, be honest with yourself. What is going on in your heart? Are you really concerned about your teenager, or are you more concerned about your reputation with your peers? It's important to check your motivation. Make sure that your reason for correcting your teen is his restoration rather than a payback for the embarrassment he has caused you.

Get to the root of the problem. Drugs and drinking are not the real problem; they are merely a symptom of something else, usually stemming from low self-esteem or a need to be accepted by peers. Use this circumstance as an opportunity to show your love to your teen. Hold him close and look into his eyes. Let him know how much you love him and how precious he is to you. This can be an incredible turning point in your relationship and will strengthen your communication with him.

Finally, remember that prayer works! God does answer prayer—you can count on it. The problem comes from failing to ask God to enter into the situation or from failing to believe God will do what we ask. It is not prayer that changes things. Rather, it is believing prayer that moves the hand of God: "And whatever things you ask in prayer, believing, you will receive" (Matt. 21:22 NKJV). According to this verse, receiving comes from two things: asking and believing. Once we have this in order, we will see the power of God released in our circumstances.

God is on your side; you are not alone. Get your pastor, prayer partners, and close friends involved. Share your teen's situation with friends who will not gossip, with those who will pray and stand with you in faith. Find people that have gone through what you are going through and have come out victorious. When you talk to them, it will encourage you. You are going to make it.

Affirmation: *God is on my side. He is working in my teen, delivering him from all drug and alcohol addiction. God answers my every prayer for my teenager because I believe God will move when I pray. My teen is delivered and set free, praise God!*

Affirmation Scriptures:
Romans 12:1–2; Matthew 21:22; 2 Timothy 2:25–26; and James 1:12.

43

Your Teen and Sexual Purity

GOD'S WORD has a lot to say about sex. He made sex a wonderful thing, and it is great—inside of marriage. But once it moves outside the confines of marriage, sex becomes disobedience and opens us up to all sorts of problems ranging from heartache and depression to terminal, sexually transmitted diseases. God's standards are not only right, they are also smart:

> Do you not know that the unrighteous will not inherit the kingdom of God? Do not be deceived. Neither *fornicators,* nor idolaters, nor *adulterers,* nor *homosexuals,* nor *sodomites,* nor thieves, nor covetous, nor drunkards, nor revilers, nor extortioners will inherit the kingdom of God. And such were some of you. But you were washed, but you were sanctified, but you were justified in the name of the Lord Jesus and by the Spirit of our God. (1 Cor. 6:9–11 NKJV, emphasis mine)

Four out of the ten things that God seeks to protect us from deal specifically with the area of sexual immorality. They include fornication, adultery, homosexuality, and sodomy.

Jesus Christ came to set us free from sin, so the best way to avoid these sins is to never get started. But if you are reading this and realize that you or your teen is already bound up in any of these areas, keep in mind that no sin is too difficult for God. Let's take another look at the last part of that previous Scripture. The *New Living Translation* says it this way:

> There was a time when some of you were just like that [*practicing these lifestyles*], but now your sins have been washed away, and you have been set apart for God. You have been made right with God because of what the Lord Jesus Christ and the Spirit of our God have done for you. (1 Cor. 6:11 NLT)

The people about whom the apostle Paul wrote had immoral lifestyles at one time or another, but God still set them free. The devil will lie to you and your teenager, telling you it's too late, that your child has gone too far for His help. But God will meet you and your teen right where you are. Even if someone is bound up by sexual immorality, there is still hope. There is always hope!

Of course, our goal as parents is to prevent our children from ever getting involved with an immoral lifestyle. We don't have to sit and watch our children fall into these sex traps; we can take definite steps to help prevent them from doing so.

One way that parents can help prevent their teens from getting involved in sexual immorality is to talk to them about sex. If they don't, someone else will. Parents usually ask me, "What's the best age to talk to your children about sex?" The best time to have the talk is *when they ask*. If you're unwilling to talk to them about it, their peers—warped morals and all—will be more than happy to share their ideas about sex with your child. It's best if your children's ideas about sex come from you rather than from another teenager. And the rule is: Sex is great in the confines of marriage. But outside of it, sex will destroy.

Be an example of sexual purity to your teen. Your lifestyle has a huge influence on her. Remember the saying, "You can teach what you know, but you'll reproduce what you are." If you are watching risqué movies, hanging around friends with loose morals, and filling your mind with all sorts of ethically damaging material, your children will do the same. On the other hand, when you make a stand for righteousness, you also inspire your children to make a stand. If there are things you refuse to watch on television or certain types of people with whom you will not be buddy-buddy, let your kids know why. It will have a huge impact on their lives, because you will be a living example to them of godly sexual behavior.

Know the kind of people your children hang around with. I once heard that a horticulturist could take a leaf from any tree in the world and tell you a number of things about the tree from the condition of that leaf alone. He could tell you from what kind of tree the leaf fell, the age of the tree, and the general health of the tree. Like adults, teenagers can say the right things and put on the right face, but it's important to watch the "leaves" they drop behind. Bill Shuler, my friend and a former campus pastor at Oral Roberts University, says, "Show me who you are hanging around, and I'll show you what you'll become." We want to make sure our teens are around positive influences.

Pray for the sexual purity of your teenager. My mother-in-law prayed her children out of so many relationships that it is amazing. Prayer is such a powerful force, but we usually make it the last line of defense for our children. We can head off a lot of stuff at the pass if we consistently pray for our children. As a parent, God has given you spiritual jurisdiction over your teenager, more so than anyone else. We need to take our spiritual authority and appropriate it.

Be sure to talk to your teenager about her relationships with the opposite sex. I am amazed at how many people are actually afraid to talk to their teens. The other day in the grocery store, a mother introduced her teenager to my wife. They began a conversation, and my wife quickly found out that the girl had a boyfriend. She asked the girl what kind of boy he was; was he a gentleman? Did she kiss on the first date? The daughter was smiling, excitedly answering all her questions and thrilled that an adult showed interest in her life. The mother turned red and said to my wife, "I could never ask my daughter those kind of questions."

"Oh, you should," my wife said, smiling, "and a whole lot more." Talk to your teenager and find out what she is thinking and doing. Then you can be of help to her.

Affirmation: *Thank You, Father, that my children flee from every form of sexual immorality. I also thank You for setting them free from any sexual sin in which they have already gotten involved. Because the cross of Christ is able to set even the vilest of sinners free, I know that You can and will deliver my children from all sexual sin. I seek to set a godly example through what I watch and listen to and how I live. My example encourages them to set a standard of moral purity in their relationships with the opposite sex.*

Affirmation Scriptures:
1 Thessalonians 4:3; Ephesians 6:10; 1 Timothy 4:12; and 1 Corinthians 3:16–17.

44

How to Prevent Teen Pregnancy

IT IS AMAZING to think about how often we are bombarded with sexually loaded material by the media. Every time we turn on the television, surf the Internet, or drive by a roadside billboard, we see sexually oriented material advertising everything from chicken wings to chow mein. The media powers that be have waged an all-out war on traditional standards regarding sex and morality. A number of today's television shows have teenagers involved in premarital sex. Because teens tend to idolize and emulate the role models they see on television, these programs can exert considerable negative influence on the sexual habits of our young people.

Although parents need to be prepared to deal with teen pregnancy, it is even more important that parents be prepared to prevent it. We are not helpless in this battle, as the world would have us believe. We do not have to capitulate and accept that our teens are going to engage in premarital sex. God wants us as parents to help our teens remain chaste and avoid sexual activity before marriage. The following suggestions are some practical things parents can do to help their teenagers resist promiscuity and say no to sex.

Set a curfew for your teenager. My grandfather always told my mother to be back home the same day she went out. Through interviewing teenage girls who have gotten pregnant, I have come to realize how wise my grandfather's advice really was. Many of the teens with whom I spoke became pregnant after midnight. Having an established curfew may have helped to prevent it from happening.

Restrict dating to group or double dating until your teen is mature enough to deal with all the emotions and physical attractions that accompany adolescence. Teenagers experience a flux of new hormones and emotions that they are not prepared to deal with. Letting them spend time alone with members of the opposite sex places them in a position of unnecessary temptation. If they are never alone together, it will be practically impossible for them to engage in premarital sex. This simply gives them a little extra time to mature until they are ready to deal with sexual temptation on their own. At the age of eighteen, many young people leave home to go off to college. At that point, it will no longer be practical for you to try to restrict their dating habits.

Encourage your teen to get to know members of the opposite sex as friends rather than jumping right into a dating relationship. Personally, I am not even convinced that the traditional form of dating is scriptural. Developing such friendships will allow your teenager to have fun and learn how the opposite sex thinks without the entanglement of a physical relationship.

Teach your teenagers that they can say no. Not only do they have the right to say no to sex, but they also have the right to say no to any type of physical involvement, including kissing or holding hands. Teenagers often get involved in physical relationships with members of the opposite sex because they feel that it is expected of them. They see everyone else doing it and feel pressure from their peers to do the same. Parents need to teach their children that they can dare to be different.

I know a woman who, when she was sixteen, realized that she had the right to say no to kissing. She had just started dating a young Christian man who really liked to kiss. Although all of her friends seemed to think nothing of it, she just wasn't comfortable with this aspect of their relationship. After several dates, she decided to break it off. She was so relieved to be out from under that pressure that she didn't even miss going out with him. She realized that she was not obligated to kiss anyone, even if she was dating him. Learning that lesson helped her through the rest of her high school years and college, preventing her from getting involved in unhealthy relationships. All because she realized that she could say no.

Now that may not sound like a big deal to you, but that's where it starts. Kids don't just jump into premarital sex. They start with kissing and getting close. Then, before they know it, they cross the line and find themselves having sex with someone.

The time for your teenager to make a quality decision not to participate in sexual immorality is not when she is in the backseat of a car down a country road or alone at a friend's house. It is before she ever gets to that point. Talk to her ahead of time. Help her to make a firm decision to resist sexual temptation before she ever gets into that situation. Most of all, help her to see how important it is to avoid temptation in the first place. Remember: "An ounce of prevention is worth a pound of cure."

You also need to let your teenager know that an unplanned pregnancy can permanently alter her life. God tells us that "my people are destroyed for lack of knowledge" (Hos. 4:6 KJV). One main reason teens go "too far" is a failure to think their actions all the way through. They probably have never even thought about being the mother or father of a little child. Parents need to talk to their teenagers, to help them consider the potential consequences of engaging in premarital sex. I have one friend who took his son on a camping trip to do just that, to talk about the risk of an unplanned pregnancy if his son had sex before marriage.

Talk to your teen about the dangers of sexually transmitted diseases. It is a common fallacy that certain forms of birth control, such as condoms, are 100 percent effective in preventing the spread of AIDS and other sexually transmitted diseases. There is still at least a 17 percent margin of risk involved.[1] Those are pretty poor odds. Help her to see that it's just not worth the risk. Abstinence is the only 100-percent effective form of protection.

Having sex with multiple partners has been linked to cervical cancer, pelvic inflammatory disease, and sexually transmitted diseases.[2] Parents need to let their teens know that the only safe lifestyle is one either of chastity or engaging in a monogamous relationship with a monogamous spouse within the confines of marriage.

Pray for your teenager when she goes out with friends. My mother-in-law prayed my wife out of many relationships with other guys before we were married. It will amaze you to discover the spiritual jurisdiction that parents have over their teenagers when they pray. Ask God to protect your teen from any person, place, or thing that may cause her harm. God commands us, "Be anxious for nothing, but in everything by prayer and supplication, with thanksgiving, let your requests be made known to God" (Phil. 4:6 NKJV). When you pray, believing, it really does change things!

Ask your teen questions about the time she spends with her friends. I am amazed at how many parents fail to ask their teenagers what they do when they go out. Parents need to be interested in their children because if they are not interested, someone else will be. Showing interest in your teen's activities communicates two things to her: (1) you are interested in what she does, and (2) you are going to be checking up on her to ensure that she behaves appropriately when she goes out. Knowing these two things will help motivate her to do the right thing when she is out with her friends.

Meet her friends. You will be astonished at what you can learn about your child from her friends. There is so much truth to the saying, "If you will show me who your teen hangs around, I will show you what he will become." What we hang around is what we will become. Your teen's friends will influence the direction of her life. "Can two people walk together without agreeing on the direction?" (Amos 3:3 NLT). The Word also says, "Do not be misled: 'Bad company corrupts good character'" (1 Cor. 15:33 NIV).

Invite her friends over to your house and get to know them. Talk to them about their goals, desires, and dreams and ask questions about their backgrounds and families. Tell them about your family and its standards. Seek to be a godly influence in their lives. In doing so, you will influence your teen's behavior as well.

Finally, help your teenager to see the benefits of purity, to catch a vision for her life unhindered by premarital sex or its consequences. Setting high goals can help a teen avoid all kinds of ungodly behavior because it gives her a reason to live right. Not only will it affect her life before marriage; it can also affect her relationship with her future spouse. Remaining chaste until she is married will help her to enter marriage with no regrets and no memories.

Affirmation: *Thank You, Lord, that I communicate clearly to my teenager the benefits of purity and the dangers presented by engaging in premarital sex. My teen has a vision for her life free from the entanglements of sexual immorality and its consequences. She avoids situations that place her in a position of temptation and develops friendships with other young people who seek to live a life of sexual purity.*

Affirmation Scriptures:
Philippians 4:8; Romans 13:14; Galatians 5:24; and 2 Corinthians 10:5.

When it comes to the decision of who will take responsibility for raising the baby, you have several options:

Adoption by another family. I have seen the joy an adopted child can bring to the lives of a husband and wife who are unable to have children. There is no shortage of childless couples who are longing for a baby to love.

Temporary adoption by the grandparents. I have also seen the parents of the teenager adopt the child until the teen is mature enough to care for it properly. This can provide a transition period for the teen parent, allowing her to grow up before taking on a huge responsibility for which she is not yet ready.

Teen parenting. This is an eye-opening, huge responsibility for a teenager. Although some teens are ready for this kind of responsibility, most are not. And even though the teen can parent the child, she will still need and should receive your help as a grandparent and parent.

Should my child marry because he or she is involved in a pregnancy? Just because a young woman is pregnant and a young man has fathered a child does not mean she or he should automatically get married. Each of the teen parents needs to answer these questions before making a lifelong commitment:

- Do they want to spend the rest of their lives with each other?
- Will he or she be a good parent to the baby?
- Are both parties mature enough for marriage? Are they ready for this commitment? It could be the right person but the wrong timing.
- Is the baby's father capable of providing financially for the new mother and baby?

If the teen father is not ready to support the baby and new mom, he needs to ask himself how he can become ready. This responsibility to help financially exists regardless of whether he marries the child's mother.

"John" and "Karen" were college sweethearts who suddenly found themselves facing the challenge of an unplanned pregnancy. After breaking the news to her mom and dad, Karen went home to have the baby. At first John "headed for the hills." It was not long before he realized his absence was a mistake and he came back to take responsibility for his actions. But by the time he came around, Karen did not want anything to do with him.

Determined to care for his unborn child, John began sending her a percentage of his paycheck to help with pregnancy expenses. Even after the baby was born, John faithfully supported Karen and the baby. His faithfulness eventually softened her heart toward him and now they are happily married with a beautiful family.

Make use of available resources. Although some families are able to provide financially for the needs of their pregnant teen, many are not. If you are in need of a little support, your local crisis pregnancy center is a good place to start. These centers can often provide free maternity clothes, baby clothes, formula, or even baby furniture. They can also help you link up with other help agencies.

Remember that God loves happy endings. We have a couple in our church who conceived a child while attending a Christian high school. Because of the pregnancy, the Christian school expelled the girl. But this young couple didn't give up; they were determined to turn their situation around. They got married, graduated from a public high school, obtained employment, and had another child. Now they have a great marriage. They have also become key leaders in our church. Remember that premarital sex is not the unpardonable sin. God is a God of restoration; He is the Master of taking bad situations and turning them around into something beautiful.

Affirmation: *Thank You for helping my child to make wise and godly decisions, to turn away from premarital sex and live a holy and chaste life. I thank You that my teen feels comfortable talking to me about any situation, including those involving premarital sex and pregnancy. As parents, we set our hearts on helping our teen make it victoriously through any* *challenges he or she may encounter in life. Our children are confident of our love and support and are not afraid to talk to us about any problem they may have.*

Affirmation Scriptures:

Philippians 4:13; Romans 8:37; Jeremiah 29:11; and Proverbs 3:5–6.

46

Homosexuality and Your Teenager

"JILL" CAME HOME one day, sat her parents down and said, "I've got to tell you something. I've been living a lie," she admitted. "It's time for me to come out of the closet. I'm a lesbian, and you're going to have to accept that, because that's the way it is."

Jill's parents were shocked, numb, and in general disbelief. They asked themselves, "How could this happen in our own family? In someone else's family, yes, but not here at our house."

This was an upper-middle-class family with good morals, a family in which the parents showed lots of love for their children. So what went wrong? They discovered that a neighbor boy had molested Jill when she was eleven years old. She had never shared this traumatic experience with her parents because she thought they would be upset with her. Instead, she suppressed her hurt and soon began to resent all boys. Through a series of events, she then convinced herself that she was destined to be a homosexual.

Homosexuality is an ever-increasing issue in America today. It is splashed all over the media, from news programs to Hollywood films and newspapers to magazines. It's even showing up in our own families. In recent years, several mainline denominations have abandoned the standard of God's Word and have advocated a gay Christian lifestyle. But what does God say about it, and is there hope for someone bound up by homosexuality?

God's Word is very clear when it comes to homosexuality. His intention for human sexual relationships is limited to heterosexual union between man and woman within the parameters of marriage (Gen. 1:27–28; 2:18, 23–24). God's plan is for us to be one flesh in marriage, male and female united. But the problem is that sin has perverted society's perspective on healthy sexuality, changing it into something very different from what God intended (Rom. 1:18–32). Blinded by the deceptiveness of modern thought on human sexuality, many are falling into destructive and sexually immoral lifestyles: God tells us, "many will follow their destructive ways, because of whom the way of truth will be blasphemed. By covetousness they will exploit you with deceptive words" (2 Peter 2:2–3 NKJV). The good news is that there is hope for anyone who has gotten caught up in this web of deception and bondage. God's unlimited power can bring healing, restoration, and deliverance because He is fully able to intervene in any person's life: "For the law of the Spirit of life in Christ Jesus has made me free from the law of sin and death" (Rom. 8:2 NKJV).

You must understand that, according to God's Word, no one is born gay (see Rom. 1:26–27). Homosexuality is a choice made by certain individuals and has nothing at all to do with genetics.

Today, many psychologists are successfully treating homosexuality. They are "changing [their patient's] sexual orientation from homosexual to heterosexual," says Charles Socarides, president of the National Association for Research and Therapy of Homosexuality (an organization uniting therapists and other professionals who believe homosexuality is not inborn and can be changed). "Such a change would be unthinkable," Socarides concludes, "if there were any truth at all to the biological or hereditary causation of homosexuality."[1] John Paulk, a homosexuality and gender specialist, says there are five main reasons why people enter into a homosexual lifestyle:

1. Early sexual abuse or violation

2. Emotional detachment from the same-sex parent

3. Cross-gender identification

4. Poor gender role modeling

5. Peer degradation

But parents can do something about it, even if their teenager has already gotten involved in homosexuality. The following keys will help parents to bring their teen back home from a homosexual lifestyle.

Number one, do not freak out. You need to keep in mind that homosexuality is not the unforgivable sin. Whenever a person repents of his sin and turns to God, he receives forgiveness and a fresh start (see 1 Cor. 6:9–11; Isa. 53:6; and 1 John 1:9). Even homosexuality is not too difficult for God to handle. Remember that we have all been involved in sinful lifestyles of one type or another: "For all have sinned and fall short of the glory of God" (Rom. 3:23 NKJV).

Second, realize that the root is rejection. At the core of the homosexual struggle, there is a deep-seated sense of rejection. Teens caught up in a homosexual lifestyle may feel rejected by their peers, by society as a whole, or even by God. They may also feel rejected by you as their parents. To push them away now would only reinforce that sense of rejection and increase their feelings of isolation. You need to assure them of your unchangeable love for them. Remember that you are God's representative. If they can be assured of your love, it can help them accept the fact that God still loves them and wants to help them overcome.

Third, pray. Ask the Lord to open a door of communication. Seek to get a dialogue going between you and your teen. If he knows he can share his struggle with you, he may be more receptive to hearing your thoughts on the issue as well. It can also provide you with some keen insights into the root source of his battle with homosexuality so that you can help him to overcome. Open communication will give you the opportunity to share God's Word with him, to encourage him about the power of God to deliver him out of homosexuality.

Number four, be honest. One thing that makes Jesus so approachable is that He understands and knows what it's like to be tempted in everything. Being honest with your teen about your own personal struggles and temptations will break down large barriers between you: "This High Priest of ours understands our weaknesses, for he faced all of the same temptations we do, yet he did not sin" (Heb. 4:15 NLT).

Next, accept him as a person, not as a thing. Remember that rejection led him down this road. Thus, it is essential that you express love and commitment to your teenager in order to help him (see 1 John 4:9–10).

Key number six: Hang on to your faith. The situation is not hopeless. You can instill hope for change. In discussing various sins, including homosexuality, Paul said,

> There was a time when some of you were just like that, but now your sins have been washed away, and you have been set apart for God. You have been made right with God because of what the Lord Jesus Christ and the Spirit of our God have done for you. (1 Cor. 6:11 NLT)

Thousands of men and women have overcome homosexuality and are able to lead sexually pure and fulfilled lives.

Also, keep consistent in your love for him. Love will cover a multitude of sins, and it will always prevail. Walk in compassion for him as he struggles against sin. Show him your loving support of his efforts to throw off the shackles of sin:

> Don't forget about those in prison. Suffer with them as though you were there yourself. Share the sorrow of those being mistreated, as though you feel their pain in your own bodies. (Heb. 13:3 NLT)

Finally, check out Christian help organizations. You may want to seek help from Christian ministries specializing in helping homosexuals leave the gay lifestyle and resume a normal heterosexual life. One national referral organization finding considerable success in this area is Exodus International. Your home church may also be able to point you to some local outreach ministries to homosexuals in your city or region.

So don't give up—you can help your child overcome any bondage, including homosexuality. God's ability to forgive and cleanse us is greater than the hold of any sin. Your love, combined with God's power, will work miracles.

Affirmation: *My child has a healthy identification with his own gender and a firm emotional attachment to both of his parents. All sexually unhealthy or homosexual ties are broken and permanently severed from his life. Thank You, Lord, for preserving my child from sexually perverse relationships and people. Our teen communicates openly and honestly with us because he is secure in knowing that we love him unconditionally and will help him through any situation he may encounter.*

Affirmation Scriptures:
Philippians 1:9; John 8:32; and Ephesians 4:24.

47

Pornography

WHAT DO YOU DO when you catch your child with a pornographic magazine or discover that he has been surfing sexually explicit Web pages on the Internet? First of all, you need to understand that pornography is a multibillion-dollar business. According to *U.S. News & World Report*, the pornography industry in the United States grossed an estimated eight billion dollars in 1996 alone. Now, if you divide out that amount to reflect individual spending, it represents an expenditure of around thirty dollars per person.[1] That figure exceeds annual spending in the U.S. on all forms of gambling combined.[2]

Pornography is an addictive bondage, but it can be broken by the power of the Holy Spirit. The best time to nip it in the bud is before it ever has the chance to get started (or at least when first detected). We must have a battle plan if we are going to fight pornography effectively and thwart its attack on our children.

In the United States, it has been estimated that approximately one in three girls and one in seven boys will be sexually molested before the age of eighteen.[3] Psychologists have discovered a strong relationship between the use of pornography and sexual child abuse. Seventy-seven percent of those who molested boys and eighty-seven percent of those who molested girls said they used hard-core pornography on a regular basis.[4]

It's a fact that pornography affects preteens as well as teens. We can see this truth clearly illustrated in the story of one young man who spent two hours in his pastor's study repeatedly calling a dial-a-porn message service. Through this, he exposed himself to a variety of sexually active phone conversations. Two weeks later, after his encounter with dial-a-porn, this twelve-year-old boy sexually assaulted a four-year-old girl.

Pornography has launched an all-out attack on our teenage boys, seeking to grab a permanent foothold in their lives. Both of the national commissions appointed to study the effects of pornography in the U.S. agree that adolescent males, ages twelve to seventeen, are among the largest consumer groups of pornography today.[5]

As a Christian parent, you can do several things to help break the power of pornography over your child. The best way to attack any spiritual problem is with your own spiritual weaponry. In Ephesians, the Bible describes the weapons God has given us for our warfare and shows us how to put these weapons into practice: "Praying always with all prayer and supplication in the Spirit, being watchful to this end with all perseverance and supplication for all the saints" (Eph. 6:18 NKJV). Because God's armor is activated through prayer, the power of God will be released in your teenager's life the moment you begin to pray for him.

In 1 John 5:16, God gives us specific instructions on how to pray. This verse tells us that "if anyone sees his brother sinning a sin which does not lead to death, he will ask, and He will give him life for those who commit sin not leading to death" (NKJV). As you begin to pray that God's life will surround and envelop your teenager, you will begin to see a softening of his heart, a new receptivity to God's presence, and a desire to be free from all bondage.

Once you have prayed for your teenager, the next thing you must do is lovingly confront him about the pornography. It is important not to sweep the problem under the rug, because it will not go away by itself. One of the greatest deceptions parents can fall into is to assume that the problem will disappear if they ignore it. Ignoring problems will not cause them to disappear. It may camouflage them for a short while, but they will eventually come to light. Thus, it is essential that you *lovingly* confront your teenager about the pornography as soon as possible. But be sure to do it lovingly, because your attitude will greatly affect the outcome of your confrontation: "Dear friends, if a Christian is overcome by some sin, you who are godly should gently and humbly help that person back onto the right path. And be careful not to fall into the same temptation yourself" (Gal. 1:6 NLT). In correcting your children, you need to have a gentle and humble attitude. You must understand that your teenager will feel embarrassed and humiliated when you approach him about this. He will probably experience a great deal of shame not only for what he has done, but also for being caught doing it. You will need to affirm him, reassuring him of your unconditional love and your desire for only what is best for his life.

This type of confrontation provides an excellent opportunity for you to share the negative effects of your own personal experiences (or those of other family members) with pornography. If you and your family are blessed enough to have avoided an encounter with pornography, you may know of a friend who has experienced the harmful effects of this insidious evil. Sharing the negative effects of pornography from personal experience will help you show your teenager that pornography has many victims and far-reaching effects.

Remember that pornography hurts not only those who view it; it also has the potential to inflict the pain of sexual abuse on innocent children. Parents cannot afford to ignore its use by their teenagers. Its negative effects are too serious and extensive. So take up your spiritual weaponry and stand in the gap: "For the weapons of our warfare are not carnal, but mighty through God to the pulling down of strong holds" (2 Cor. 10:4 KJV). Break any addictive hold that pornography has on your teen. Most of all, keep your heart right. Speak the truth in love and believe God for the victory.

Affirmation: *Thank You, Lord, for surrounding my children with the protection of the Holy Spirit. You keep them safe from pornography and from all those who use it. Child molesters and other sex offenders do not come near them. My children stay far from pornographic materials, filling their minds instead with Your Word and those things that are pure and clean. In the name of Jesus, I break the hold of pornography over my children and ask for Your cleansing of their thoughts and memories.*

Affirmation Scriptures:

Job 31:1; Psalm 101:3; Philippians 4:8; and Titus 2:12.

48

Communicating with Your Teenager

REMEMBER HOW EXCITED you were to see your little boy put together words when he was two, form sentences at three, and speak in full-blown paragraphs at the age of four? Then he hit puberty, and you found yourself wondering whatever happened to that precious little boy? It seems as though he digressed into Neanderthal man. Now he grunts, points, and uses indefinable one-syllable words. You probably wouldn't even raise an eyebrow if you saw him through your back window crouching over a pile of rocks, wearing an animal skin loincloth and rubbing two sticks together. You only pray your neighbor's cat, Fifi, doesn't wander into the backyard while your son's there; he might suddenly decide to "capture" a new loincloth or grill a couple of Fifi burgers.

But when your girl hits puberty, something quite different transpires. She talks and continues to talk. When you think she's done talking, she just keeps on going. The Energizer bunny has nothing on her! It's almost as though she can talk without taking a breath. Dumbfounded, you go to the computer to discover more about this amazing phenomenon. Finding nothing, you come up with your own prognosis called *snout sentencing*, the actual breathing of air in through the nose and forming of words out of the mouth simultaneously. Your daughter has defied the natural laws of breathing!

You discover that the telephone has become an extension of her ear. She holds the phone with her neck for days at a time without ever straightening her head, causing you to wonder whether the bones of her neck are fusing off to the side. If she thinks something, it comes out of her mouth. No filtering system here. Most of the time, you have no idea what she's saying. It's like watching a foreign film without the captions. You can identify certain words, but they don't seem to go together. But her friends are apparently communicating in the same manner, so you're not alarmed. You think it's normal.

For fear of being rejected, many teenage boys do not feel the freedom to ask questions, share emotions, or voice their opinions when they are around their peers. They don't want to look dumb in front of their friends. Girls, on the other hand, are more into airing their views, right or wrong. They love dialoguing.

I have discussed this observation with some of my friends who teach high school. They are quick to point out the difference in thought processes between boys and girls. Boys want to conquer, whereas girls just like to communicate. The teacher asks the question, "Who was the first man to walk on the face of the moon?" The boy thinks he knows the answer, and his hand confidently goes up. The teacher calls on him. His answer? "Louis Armstrong!" The teacher bursts out laughing, and suddenly the class begins to laugh too. Some other guys start to shout out words like *moron, cheese brain,* and *ozone warrior.* You can be sure that the boy's hand won't go back up for another decade.

Now the same question is asked, and a girl lifts her hand. Called on to speak, she boldly answers, "Buzz Lightyear." "Wrong!" the teacher responds. The girl's hand goes up again and again and again. She will not quit until she has exhausted every name she knows. Her objective is to communicate.

It seems almost unthinkable, but we were once the same way. How did we forget what Fifi burgers taste like or lose the art of snout sentencing? If you're one of those blessed people with parents who are still living, ask them about it. Watch the corners of their mouths climb upward and bloom into a full-blown grin.

So, with all this age-related communication going on, how do we as parents learn to effectively communicate with our teenagers? Although you may not use the same vocabulary they do, you can still do some things to help strengthen the communication link with your teen.

First, you need to encourage her. She needs to see that rejection of her ideas does not equal rejection of her personally. If your teen suggests something so far out in left field that even Mark McGwire could not come close, don't spew out at her, "That's the dumbest idea I've ever heard!" A better approach would be, "That's really interesting. I don't think I would have ever thought of that, but I was thinking more like . . ." Doing this will help your teen separate her self-image from her ideas, making it easier for her to share new "great ideas" with you in the future.

Give her feedback. Children need feedback from their parents, both positive and negative. Let them know what you're thinking, but remember to use tact—their little egos are tender. Always keep in mind that we're talking about communication here; our goal is not to point out all the flaws in our children! Communication must always be tempered and guided by love. And that love will cover a multitude of sins.

Finally, stay connected with God. You may wonder how this relates to improving communication with your teen, but it does. You will be amazed at the direct effect your relationship with God has on your communication with your child: "But if we walk in the light as He is in the light, we have fellowship with one another" (1 John 1:7 NKJV). When our fellowship with the Lord is good, it directly affects our fellowship with others, especially with the members of our family. When we talk openly about our concerns with the Lord and quit trying to show our self-sufficiency, we allow Him to get involved in those problem areas. And He wants to be a part of them. It's amazing how staying connected with God will enhance your communication with your teen, promoting true fellowship between you.

Affirmation: *Thank You, Father, that our teen is comfortable sharing her ideas and experiences with us because she feels love and support from us as her parents. Our communication link is strong and active. Employing sensitivity and tact in our responses, we seek to provide her with honest feedback. We set our hearts to building her up and not tearing her down, to showing love without condition.*

Affirmation Scriptures:

James 1:19; Proverbs 1:5; and Isaiah 54:13.

49

Eating Disorders and Your Teenager

EATING DISORDERS, especially among American girls, are escalating at an alarming rate. One percent of teenage girls and five percent of college-age women in the United States today suffer from anorexia nervosa (self-starvation) and/or bulimia nervosa (binge eating and self-induced vomiting).[1]

These disorders can have extremely dangerous effects. In fact, *U.S. News & World Report* claims that anorexia has the highest mortality rate of all mental illnesses. People bound by these disorders risk insomnia, depression, erosion of the teeth and gums, heart and kidney damage, intestinal ulcers, and changes in or loss of menstrual cycles.[2] This is serious business. But the good news is that the bondage of eating disorders can be broken.

According to psychologist Dr. Laura Lees, an expert in eating disorders, the three primary reasons for anorexia and bulimia are cultural pressure, biology, and poor family dynamics.[3] Applying tremendous social pressure, the media and society in general have put unrealistic expectations on our teenagers. Think about this: The average American woman is 5'4" and weighs over 140 pounds, while most supermodels are 5'10" and weigh just over 110 pounds.[4] This kind of cultural pressure causes many girls to begin dieting as young as ten years old.[5]

Research shows that most people suffering from eating disorders come from affluent families. Those who live in families experiencing divorce, marital problems, domestic violence, or a death in the family have evidenced a special vulnerability.[6]

Experts also claim that eating disorders evolve from a deep desire to be in control. When the outside world seems to be spinning out of control, the bulimic or anorexic develops a strong desire to control the world inside.[7] According to Dr. James Dobson, a well-known psychologist and expert on the family, both anorexia and bulimia represent a strong desire for control of one's life. The typical anorexia patient is a compliant female in late adolescence or early adulthood. A well-behaved child, she keeps her anger and frustration—at being powerless while growing up—inside her. Then one day she manifests her need for control through a serious eating disorder. She needs at least one area over which she can be the boss. Individuals with eating disorders usually view being overweight as a cause of ridicule and hatred by peers.

Perfectionist expectations from parents can also lead to eating disorders.[8] In this type of family, parents often try to project a perfect image to the outside world. They maintain strict standards of cleanliness and forbid children to make a mess of any kind. Prohibiting children from expressing disagreement, these parents don't allow their children to discuss their real feelings. In a perfectionist environment, children often feel they have to earn their parents' love.

Parents need to assure their children that they love them for who they are and not for what they do. This unconditional love accurately reflects God's love for all of us. Ephesians 1:6 tells us that "He made us accepted in the Beloved" (NKJV). We do not have to earn or work for that acceptance—we have already received it. Even so, many adults still try to earn acceptance from God the same way children try to earn love from their parents. As parents, we need to set an example of unconditional acceptance. Like our heavenly Father, we need to accept our children for who they are and not for what they do.

Major warning signs of an eating disorder include excessive use of laxatives, refusal to eat when hungry, excessive weight loss, compulsive solitary exercising, and constant weighing several times a day. The anorexic and/or bulimic may make statements like, "I'm so fat" that have no basis in fact. They may also show perfectionism in other areas of their lives such as appearance, grades, sports, neatness, and organization. Teens with eating disorders may spend a lot of time in the bathroom (especially after meals), change their wardrobe, dress in layers to hide increasing thinness, wear heavy sweaters and warm clothes in the summertime, and stay consistently cold.[9]

You can do a number of things to help your teen overcome an eating disorder. The following keys will help you provide her with the support she needs to recover.

Number one, help your teenager see herself as God sees her. The children of Israel were hindered in receiving their inheritance by an inability to see themselves as capable of obtaining God's promises. Numbers 13:33 tells us that when the Israelites came to the promised land, they saw giants living there. Instead of believing God would help them defeat their enemies, they compared themselves to the giants and became like grasshoppers in their own minds. Because the Israelites viewed themselves this way, the inhabitants of the land also came to see the Israelites as grasshoppers. Their perceptions became reality; they became what they believed themselves to be. The following Scriptures will help your child to see herself as God sees her and avoid the trap of the Israelites:

We are more than conquerors through Him who loved us. (Rom. 8:37 NKJV)

I can do all things through Christ who strengthens me. (Phil. 4:13 NKJV)

He is a new creation; old things have passed away; behold, all things have become new. (2 Cor. 5:17 NKJV)

We [have] become the righteousness of God in Him. (2 Cor. 5:21 NKJV)

The way that your child sees herself is extremely important because "as he thinks in his heart, so is he" (Prov. 23:7 NKJV).

Key number two is to help your teen understand that *you* accept her without condition. Again, we have been made accepted in the "Beloved" (Eph. 1:6). Knowing that you accept her unconditionally will help prevent your teen from being performance oriented in her relationships with others and with God.

The third key is to resist the enemy's attack over your teenager. Take your stand as a parent and actively come against the devil. Remember that anorexia and bulimia are trying to destroy your child. James 4:7 says, "Therefore submit to God. Resist the devil and he will flee" (NKJV). As you take spiritual authority over your child, you will see the power of God released and the anointing set her free from the eating disorder.

Finally, if you see these symptoms continue to persist, it is essential that you seek professional help for your child. Don't let your desire to appear the perfect family keep you from asking for help. Jesus said in Luke 5:31, "Those who are well have no need of a physician, but those who are sick" (NKJV). The sooner these eating disorders are discovered and dealt with, the easier it will be for your child to break through to victory.

Affirmation: *I break every bondage and eating disorder over my teen and declare her delivered and victorious in Jesus Christ! The anointing of God is released to heal her and set her free in every area of her life. Because we show her unconditional acceptance, she is secure in knowing that we love her not for what she does but for who she is.*

Affirmation Scriptures:
Romans 8:37; Philippians 4:13; and 2 Corinthians 5:21.

50

Forgiving Your Teenager

OVER THE YEARS, I have held on to a simple yet key truth another minister once shared with me: Be quick to repent and quick to forgive. Putting this directive into practice has helped me over and over again in my dealings with other people. If we walk in these two things, we can't help but live the victorious life that God has prepared for us. They are the major factors affecting all human relations, including those of parents with their children.

I remember all too clearly my own imperfections as a young man. During my teenage years, I was a mother's worst nightmare. Kicked out of three schools and addicted to drugs, I was a flunky with an attitude. I flat-out didn't care what people thought. My mom, on the other hand, was Mrs. Country Club. She involved herself in the PTA, initiated highly visible community fund-raisers, and won Mrs. Congeniality hands down. I was a blemish on her debutante image. As I look back over my life, I wonder why she didn't poison me or at least seal me up in a fifty-gallon drum and drop me deep in the Amazon rain forest, never to be seen again by civilized man! I guess no one except another mother can really understand a mother's love.

You will probably notice shortly (if you haven't already) that your teenager is not perfect either. But remember parents, neither are you. Your teen undoubtedly will do things to embarrass you, your family, and your church. Even your dog might hang his head in shame and deny that he knows your teen. Nevertheless, he is still your child. In the midst of his search for maturity, he might just goof up completely in certain areas of his life. In fact, he may even goof up two or three (hundred) times in the same area. The question is, How do you as a parent handle it when he does?

The answer is simple: forgiveness. If you don't walk in forgiveness for your kids, husband, wife, friends, and even your enemies, you will never walk in the victory God has for you. When you forgive your child, not only do you release him to change for the better, but you also release yourself from the bondage that unforgiveness always brings with it.

Jesus told the story of a man who, after having been forgiven a huge debt, refused to forgive a much smaller debt owed to him by someone else. After his master had forgiven the servant's very large debt, the servant went out and demanded immediate payment from a fellow servant who owed him a much smaller amount. Upon discovering that his fellow servant could not pay the debt, the man had him thrown into prison. When his master heard what had happened, he seized the man whose debt had been forgiven and said, "You wicked servant! I forgave you all that debt because you begged me. Should you not also have had compassion on your fellow servant, just as I had pity on you?" Angry with his servant for his stingy and unforgiving attitude, the master delivered him over to the torturers until he could pay off his entire debt (Matt. 18:27–34 NKJV).

The problem is that many Christians have turned themselves over to the torturers because they are holding unforgiveness in their hearts. Although you may have difficulty letting go of your own hurt and bitterness, do not give up. You can still do it.

Keep in mind that forgiveness is a decision, not a feeling. You may not feel all warm and fuzzy toward the person you need to forgive, but you can still do it. Forgiveness is not always easy, especially when someone has hurt you deeply. And sometimes the most difficult people to forgive are those closest to us. But we must choose to forgive if we truly want to be free.

Think about Jesus when He was hanging from the cross. I am sure He didn't feel warm and fuzzy about all the agony He was going through. Those nails hurt, and so did the wounds on His back. Even so, He chose to forgive His tormentors: "Father, forgive them; for they know not what they do" (Luke 23:34 KJV).

God never tells us to do anything that's too hard for us to actually do. His commandment to forgive others is given without qualification. We are to forgive *everyone* who sins against us, regardless of what he does. God does not permit us to be selective about who we forgive. If forgiveness were based on feeling, then forgiving everyone would indeed be impossible. But it isn't based on feeling. It's based upon a decision to forgive—it's an act of faith.

Pray for those who hurt you. It is hard to hold unforgiveness in your heart toward someone for whom you pray on a regular basis. There's something about intercessory prayer that works the miracle of forgiveness in the heart of the intercessor. When you pray for another person, it helps you see him through the eyes of God. It can give you understanding for him and for why he acts the way he does. It can also fill you with the compassion of God for that person.

If it's been obvious that you have been holding unforgiveness toward a certain person, ask him to forgive you. Only do this if you have been testy with him and your unforgiveness is obvious. Nothing feels worse than having someone ask you to forgive him for a wrong attitude toward you when you weren't even aware he had anything against you in the first place.

Make a decision to look at the good. Sometimes all you have to do to get mad is to just look at your kid. You don't like the way he chews his food, or his breathing bugs you. He never puts the toilet seat back where it belongs you're looking for things that he does to irritate you. Then one day he fails to put his toothbrush back in his cup, and you unload on him the arsenal of unforgiveness that you've been storing up for the past two years. It's essential that we focus on the good and not on the bad, especially when it comes to our families:

> And now, dear friends, let me say one more thing as I close this letter. Fix your thoughts on what is true and honorable and right. Think about things that are pure and lovely and admirable. Think about things that are excellent and worthy of praise. (Phil. 4:8 NLT)

Whenever a thought comes to mind about things in the past for which you have already forgiven your teenager, quickly ask God to bless him. It's amazing how doing this will change your heart toward him. Instead of being overcome with evil, you will overcome evil with good.

God wants us to be free from unforgiveness because nothing will hold us captive as tightly as unforgiveness. Follow the above steps and walk in the freedom God has purchased for you. Living a life of forgiveness will help you to live the victorious Christian life.

Affirmation: *I am quick to forgive and quick to repent. I rid myself completely of all unforgiveness toward my teenager and others who have hurt me. In doing so, I set my teen free to grow in God and release myself to walk in the victorious life God has planned for me.*

Affirmation Scriptures:
Philippians 4:8; Matthew 6:14; Ephesians 4:32; and 1 John 1:9.

51

How Do I Apologize to My Teenager?

MANY PARENTS HAVE a hard time apologizing to their teenagers. It's too easy to watch your kids goof up and then blame them for your outbursts of anger and hasty judgments. Parents will often condemn their children for bad behavior while making excuses for their own wrong actions. But if we want our kids to take responsibility for their actions, we must first be willing to do it ourselves.

When I was growing up, my father belonged to the school of thought that parents were incapable of being wrong. And even if the parents were wrong, they still were not considered wrong. It was as simple as that. For some reason or another, parents always had a good reason for their actions even if what they did wasn't right.

After my dad and I got saved, we agreed to do something we'd never really tried before—*work* at our relationship. We hadn't had the best of relationships while I was growing up. While my father dealt with a bankrupt company and a fresh divorce, I was busy getting into trouble with everything from substance abuse to blatant rebellion. When we came to Christ, we realized that God wanted to do a miracle in our relationship. I knew it would take some work on both our parts because we could not get along with each other for more than a few minutes at a time.

We had decided to kick off our new relationship with a camping trip to Canada. My father had been promising to take me camping since I was five years old, but had always had to postpone it because of one thing or another. After about a week of looking forward to a camping trip together, something would always happen to prevent him from leaving his business for any extended period of time, and the trip would be canceled.

I will never forget as long as I live the day that he apologized to me for the first time. He came into my bedroom, sat in my desk chair, and said, "Son, we're going to have to postpone our Canada trip. I know I told you I would take you camping, but I can't. It was wrong for me to promise you this and not be able to fulfill it. I'm sorry."

I looked up in shock and asked him to please repeat what he had just said. And he did, finishing it with the two words, "I'm sorry." I was smiling from ear to ear. He finally looked up at me and shook his head, wondering why I was smiling. I said, "Dad, this is the first time in my life that you have ever apologized to me." I will never forget how much that apology from my father meant to me. I knew that Dad was really working on our relationship; that apology was the beginning of a great breakthrough for us.

Apologizing to your child requires humility on your part. Along with that humility will come a pliable tenderness that will enhance not only your life but the lives of your family and friends as well. When you ask your child for forgiveness, there are certain things you need to keep in mind. They are key to any successful attempt at reconciliation.

Go to them; do not make them come to you. The person who commits the wrong has a responsibility to initiate reconciliation. If you broke a promise, lost your temper, or generally behaved wrongly, you need to go to your child and apologize:

> Therefore if you bring your gift to the altar, and there remember that your brother has something against you, leave your gift there before the altar, and go your way. First be reconciled to your brother, and then come and offer your gift. (Matt. 5:23–24 NKJV)

Don't make excuses for your actions; instead take responsibility for them. If you behaved wrongly, admit it. Don't try to place the blame on your child for your lack of self-control or failure to keep your word. Remember that we're all accountable to God for our own actions, regardless of what someone else does to us.

Remove the word *but* from your apology. The effect of an apology is greatly lessened by this three-letter word. All too often, a parent's apology is qualified: "I'm sorry I got angry, *but* you really made me mad." In truth, you are still blaming your child for your actions.

Let your child know how it would make you feel if she did to you what was done to her. Putting yourself in her place lets her know you understand the impact of your actions.

Look her in the eyes when you talk to her. This lets your teen know that you love her and are serious about your apology. It has been said that the eyes are the window to the soul. Looking your child in the eyes while asking for her forgiveness will communicate the depth and truth of your regret for hurting her.

Ask her to forgive you. You need to speak the words; you can't assume that your remorse is just understood. Make it clear to her in terms she can understand.

It takes a mature person to ask forgiveness. Sometimes it is easier to forgive others for their mistakes than it is to ask forgiveness from those who witness our own failures.

Affirmation: *Thank You, Lord, for the humility to admit to my children when I am wrong. Because I accept responsibility for my actions, my children also learn to accept responsibility for their own actions. They know that I take their feelings seriously and care deeply about the impact of my actions on their lives.*

Affirmation Scriptures:
Colossians 3:12; Ephesians 6:4; and Colossians 3:21.

52

Guidelines in Bringing Correction to Your Teenager

No MATTER how long we have known the Lord, we still continue to grow and mature in our walk with Him. Even Paul the Apostle, as great a Christian as he was, wrote in one of his last letters that he still had not arrived spiritually:

> I don't mean to say that I have already achieved these things or that I have already reached perfection! But I keep working toward that day when I will finally be all that Christ Jesus saved me for and wants me to be. (Phil. 3:12 NLT)

If Paul could say he had not yet reached perfection in his attitudes and actions, you can rest assured that God still has a lot of work to do on us. He is moving each one of us from one realm of glory to another. God doesn't give up on us because we mess up sometimes— He just keeps working on us. In helping us to mature, God uses these four things:

1. His Word

2. the Holy Spirit

3. circumstances

4. other people

God places people in our lives to stretch and challenge us. This stretching in turn produces maturity and a spirit of excellence in our lives. As a parent, you are called of God to be an influential force in your teen's life, to help bring him into new realms of maturity. Whether we realize it or not, God uses our teens to stretch and mature us as well. This may sound obvious at first, but it's all too easy for parents to forget the big picture when they're in the middle of a challenging situation with their kids. It is during those times of difficulty that we're tempted to lose sight of the fact that God has placed them in our lives to help us mature spiritually too.

"Only a fool despises a parent's discipline; whoever learns from correction is wise" (Prov. 15:5 NLT). We don't want our children to despise our discipline. Instead, we want them to learn and improve from it. As parents, there are certain things we can do to help our children become more receptive to discipline. Receptivity to proper discipline produces a wisdom and maturity in our children that will help them the rest of their lives.

The following keys will help prevent your teen from despising parental correction. They will make it easier for him to receive discipline from you, effect changes in his life for the better, and prevent him from becoming bitter.

Don't correct him in front of his friends or peers. I have seen many parents correct their children in front of their children's friends. Doing this goes beyond correction and moves into the realm of humiliation. If you humiliate your child, you will breach his trust and drive a wedge between you. Jesus was very clear about how to properly correct someone: "If another believer sins against you, go *privately* and point out the fault. If the other person listens and confesses it, you have won that person back" (Matt. 18:15 NLT, emphasis mine).

Don't correct him in anger. Keep in mind that one of the reasons he may frustrate you so much is that his behavior reflects some of your own tendencies. If he starts to irritate you, take a big breath, count to ten (maybe to one hundred and ten!), and let the peace of

God rule over your heart: "Therefore you are inexcusable, O man, whoever you are who judge, for in whatever you judge another you condemn yourself; for you who judge practice the same things" (Rom. 2:1 NKJV).

Give your teen positive attention; do not just communicate with your child when he does something wrong. When we were youth pastors, we had a guy in our youth group who was continually causing trouble. He disrupted our services and clowned around all the time. As I began to work with him, I realized that he wasn't getting any positive attention at home. The only time his parents talked to him was when he was in trouble for something that he did or did not do.

As his youth pastor, I began to acknowledge him for the things he did right. I praised him more for the good things he did than I criticized him for the wrong things he did. After about five months, this guy became a model leader in our youth group. Amazed, his parents asked me how I was able to keep him under control during the youth services. After I told them how I'd accomplished it, they decided to implement the same principle at home. They noticed an immediate difference in their son. People want to be noticed, and they will get attention—one way or another.

Keep in mind that the object of correction is restoration, not retribution. It's important to remember your motives for correction: You want to restore your teen and help him to be his very best. There is a definite difference between correction and punishment. God is in the restoration business, something we need to make our passion as well. As Jack Hayford says, "Restoration in every dimension of human experience is at the heart of the Christian gospel. It is woven through all the Scriptures and must be at the forefront of our ministry of the truth."[1]

Have the right spirit, not just the right words. Second Corinthians 3:6, a powerful and life-changing Scripture, tells us, "The letter kills, but the Spirit gives life" (NKJV). In this context, Paul was comparing the old covenant with the new covenant. But there is another deep truth contained in this passage: If we share truth with people but do it with a wrong heart, we will end up causing more damage than good. If we are going to be effective in correcting our teenagers, we must do it in truth and love. God tells us to speak the truth in love (Eph. 4:15). Notice that He doesn't simply *say* the truth. He says the truth *in love*. Love can make it easier to receive the truth and will cover a multitude of goof-ups.

Correcting your children with the right attitude will make it much easier for them to receive discipline from you. Remember that attitude is everything. Make sure you praise your children when they do something right; don't just correct them when they do wrong. This will help them to make good changes in their lives and to know that you want the very best for them.

Affirmation: *I correct my children with a right heart, seeking the very best for them and not simply to punish them. Knowing that I correct them with love, they respond quickly and positively to my discipline. As I respond in love to the challenges I encounter with my children, I realize the benefits of spiritual growth and maturity in my own life.*

Affirmation Scriptures:
Proverbs 22:6; Proverbs 6:23; Ephesians 6:4; and Proverbs 3:12.

53

I Can't Understand What My Teenager Is Going Through!

I AM SURE you've heard people say, "Today's teenagers face temptations we never had to face when we were growing up." I remember my own parents telling me that very thing when I was growing up, and they said their parents told it to them too. But instead of making me feel better, that statement just made me feel isolated and helpless. I figured that Mom and Dad could never begin to understand all the things I was going through, so why should I even try to talk to them about it. I concluded that I might as well just go ahead and yield to every temptation that came my way.

But that idea couldn't be farther from the truth. This attitude of new, unrelatable temptations digs an even deeper canyon between the older and younger generations. It causes people to feel that parents can't relate to kids and kids can't relate to parents. It makes them doubt they will ever be able to understand one another. But if this were true, God's Word would cease to be as relevant today as it was two thousand years ago. People overcame temptations in the days of old the same way that we overcome them today—through the Word of God. God's Word has not lost one ounce of potency or ability, and the Holy Spirit has not weakened in power over the years. In fact, where sin abounds, God declares His grace abounds even more (see Rom. 5:20).

So don't feel hopeless as a parent. Your children don't need to feel hopeless, either. We don't have to believe the myth that temptation is any different today from twenty years ago. We deal with temptation the same way now that people dealt with it back then.

Different package, same temptation. "Yeah," some say, "but they didn't have X-rated movies, drugs, drive-by shootings, television, video games, or the Internet." And the list goes on. But you would be surprised by what they did have. They faced the same old rotten stuff we face; it was just wrapped in different packaging.

We must realize that the root of every sin is selfishness. The wrapping on the outside may take various forms, such as lust, substance abuse, or murder. But when you get right down to it, every sin is the result of selfishness. That is why Jesus, when asked what the greatest commandment was, highlighted our responsibility to live by the rule of love for others: "'And you must love the Lord your God with all your heart, all your soul, all your mind, and all your strength.' The second is equally important: 'Love your neighbor as yourself.' No other commandment is greater than these" (Mark 12:30–31 NIT) Love is the opposite of selfishness. If we are to be free from sin, we have to walk in love because love covers all sins (see Prov. 10:12).

Temptation does not come from God. We will never free our children to walk in victory or be able to walk in victory ourselves if we insist on cramming down their throats the idea that God is the one who tempts us. It is true that overcoming temptation serves to strengthen us, but we need to realize that the temptation itself does not come from God. God's Word could not be any plainer on this issue: "Let no one say when he is tempted, 'I am tempted by God'; for God cannot be tempted by evil, nor does He Himself tempt anyone" (James 1:13 NKJV).

God and the devil are not on the same team. The truth is that God is good, the devil is bad, and the two are not working together to get you. God is working to help you, to guide you away from temptation. In fact, Jesus taught His disciples to pray this very thing:

"And do not lead us into temptation, / But deliver us from the evil one" (Matt. 6:13 NKJV).

Nothing is new under the sun. The same tempting stuff that Adam and Eve faced in the Garden, we face today. The same internal conflicts that Cain and Abel experienced at the dawn of civilization are the same inner struggles we go through now. And the various temptations faced centuries ago by King David and the apostles Peter, James, and John continue to challenge our faith today: "No temptation has overtaken you except such as is common to man; but God is faithful, who will not allow you to be tempted beyond what you are able, but with the temptation will also make the way of escape, that you may be able to bear it" (1 Cor. 10:13 NKJV). The only things the devil has to work with are the things that are common to man. He doesn't have any new equipment. He has the same temptations he has always had. They just come with different wrapping paper now.

If others have made it, your teen can too! When God talks to us in 1 Peter 5:9 about withstanding the enemy, He says to "resist him, steadfast in the faith" (NKJV). But He doesn't stop there. He adds this powerful statement: "knowing that the same sufferings are experienced by your brotherhood in the world." A different translation puts it this way: "Remember that Christians all over the world are going through the same kind of suffering you are" (1 Peter 5:9 NLT).

Other people deal with the same temptations you and your teenager encounter, and they come through them victoriously. It's good to know that you're not the only one having these battles. You and your teenager can overcome each attack of the enemy with the Word of God. It worked for others, and it will work for you.

Affirmation: *Thank You, Lord, that I not only understand the trials and temptations faced by my teenager, but I also have the wisdom and discernment to help her make it through victoriously. We look to the Word and to Your Spirit for our help and deliverance. The Holy Spirit is working* *powerfully within my children and me to make us strong and cause us to overcome every temptation. We put aside all selfishness and seek to walk in love for others, loving others as we love ourselves.*

Affirmation Scriptures:

Isaiah 42:16; Psalm 31:3; Psalm 32:8; and Philippians 2:13.

54

Getting Your Schedule Under Control

IN TODAY'S WORLD, it's all too easy for our priorities to get out of whack, especially with so many "good" things on which to spend our time. These good things often take the form of school, business meetings, conferences, sporting events, extracurricular activities, and even church. Now you may find it hard to believe that a pastor would say this, but it's true: The church is here for the family, not the family for the church.

God makes it clear in His Word that we are to keep our priorities straight. The Bible tells us to live purposefully and correctly, not as unwise, but as wise, sensible, intelligent people. We are to make the very most of the time, buying up each opportunity, because the days are evil (see Eph. 5:15–16).

No one, not even those in the ministry, should put the church before his family. I once heard the story of a young, enthusiastic pastor of a growing church who got so wrapped up in his ministry that he let his priorities get reversed. One day, when he felt especially excited about the growth of his church, he held up the church bulletin and waved it in front of his wife. He said, "Look honey, we've got something going on every night of the week at church!"

Apparently, his wife was not so impressed. She smiled sweetly and said, "That's nice, but don't you think it's important for our people to spend time with their families? To build strong relationships with each other as well as with the Lord?" The pastor was a little upset that his wife would ask such a question. With a scowl on his face, he answered, "Of course I think it's important. The Bible tells us that we are supposed to do that." Still smiling, the wife said, "Great. On what night of the week do you think we are supposed to spend time together?"

It's easy to get all caught up in doing good things, but we need to remember that good is not always best. Church is important, but if you spend four nights a week at church and three nights a week at basketball and football games, you will never have time to do anything with your family.

If you do not set your schedule, your schedule will set you. I don't know if you have ever opened your calendar and gotten confused just by looking at it, but it is no fun. Overscheduling often leads not only to confusion, but also to broken commitments and a lack of quality time with your family. Setting and keeping your priorities straight takes work, planning and, most of all, self-discipline.

Scheduling your family back into your life takes a little effort on your part. The following keys will help you set aside time on a regular basis to spend with your family.

First, make your family a priority. If your spouse and children are not the most important thing in your life—other than your relationship with God—you need to make some adjustments. Making those adjustments may not be easy at first, but it will pay off in ways that are invaluable. Spending time with your family is like investing in a high-interest-bearing account: The more you put in over an extended period of time, the greater the yield.

Second, write out your priorities and rank them. And be honest with yourself. An ideal priority list might look something like this: (1) God; (2) wife; (3) children; (4) job; (5) recreation. Writing down your priorities in order will provide you with a visual example of what matters most to you.

Third, write out some goals you would like to see take place in your family. Then under each goal, list some things you can do to see that goal become a reality. For example: *Goal*—Communicate better with my wife. *Things to do*—Take her out on a date once a week. Ask her about her day when I come home from work and listen to what she says.

Think of practical ways to achieve your goals. Most goals are attainable if we just take the time to discover how to reach them.

Next, go through your calendar, scheduling and planning vacations and special family times. Write down these dates in red ink with the knowledge that neither you nor your family members can touch them. These dates are "holy" days or weeks and can't be changed. Your commitment to keeping family outings must be firm, or other things will come up and bump them right back down the priority list.

Finally, give everyone the opportunity to schedule family time doing things that he or she likes. For example, my wife hates camping, but she will sacrifice by spending a night in the great outdoors because she knows that her children and husband love it. On the other hand, the children and I sacrifice by going shopping with her. For the sake of the other members of your family, you may need to do things you don't particularly enjoy. That way, family times are rewarding for every member of the family—kids and adults, male and female alike.

When your family realizes you have made them a priority, it will change the way they respond to you. Instead of feeling like an afterthought, they will feel like a real part of your life and will open up to you in ways they refused to do before. They will begin to trust you with their feelings and dreams, and you will all develop a deep sense of belonging. The knowledge that you truly belong will produce a confidence and boldness in God's purpose and destiny for your life as nothing else will.

Affirmation: *I make my family a priority in my life. Other than my relationship with God, nothing is more important to me than my spouse and children. I set aside time on a regular basis to spend with them, getting to* *know them and communicating with them on a deeply personal level. I refuse to allow other things, including my career, to take precedence over developing a solid relationship with my family.*

Affirmation Scriptures:

Ephesians 5:15–16; Matthew 25:23; and 1 Chronicles 16:11.

55

How Do I Talk to My Teen About My Ex-Spouse?

DIVORCE ISN'T FUN. There are no winners in a divorce, especially where children are concerned. That is why God hates it when families split up. Malachi 2:16 tells us, "'For the LORD God of Israel says / That He hates divorce, / For it covers one's garment with violence,' / Says the LORD of hosts. / 'Therefore take heed to your spirit, / That you do not deal treacherously'" (NKJV).

Divorce can be brutal. That's why God warns us not to get sucked into treachery. A treacherous attitude can take the form of bitterness toward your ex. Such bitterness will not only hurt you; it will also hurt your children. In Hebrews 12:15, God warns us that bitterness defiles those around us: "Lest any root of bitterness springing up trouble you, and thereby many be defiled" (KJV). We can't afford to harbor in our hearts the bitterness that so often accompanies marital separation.

Speaking ill of your ex-husband or ex-wife can backfire and damage your relationship with your child. Although you may be able to influence a younger child against your ex, you may not be so successful with an older child. Over time, children grow weary of the barrage of insults toward someone they love. A parent who seeks to turn his child against his ex-spouse will only serve to put up a barrier between himself and his child.

Charlie was twelve years old when his mom and dad got divorced. Charlie's mother was always telling him that his dad was a dirty rotten scoundrel. At first, his mother was successful, and Charlie saw his dad as the enemy. But even in the midst of this verbal attack, the father refused to speak ill about Charlie's mom. On the contrary, he always reminded Charlie that she was the only mother Charlie would ever have. His dad encouraged him to remember that his mom was very special.

As time went on, Charlie began to grow weary of hearing his mother continually lambaste his dad. Because she was dealing treacherously through her negative words about his father, his mom was inadvertently driving a wedge between herself and her son. It's easy to become vindictive and retaliatory when going through a divorce, but we have to resist it. We can't let ourselves be "overcome with evil." Instead, we are to overcome evil with good (see Rom. 12:21).

Divorce is bad, no doubt about it. But it always amazes me how God can take a bad situation and turn it into something good. He turns our scars into stars, but in order for this to happen we have to be willing to cooperate with His Word and His Spirit. You have to be willing to put God and your children first.

As a parent, your first priority will be to minimize the negative impact on your kids from the breakup of your home. A divorce will be painful to your children, but it doesn't have to be devastating. There are some things you can do to protect your child from the damaging effects of a divorce.

Pray for your ex-spouse. Matthew 5:44 says, "But I say to you, love your enemies, bless those who curse you, do good to those who hate you, and pray for those who spitefully use you and persecute you" (NKJV). The neat thing about praying for your ex-spouse is that it will not only help him or her; it will also bless you. Praying for those who have hurt you will help heal your own heart from resentment and hurt.

Be honest with God. Tell Him about the hurts and wrong attitudes you have toward your ex. Doing this will expose your bad attitudes so that God can deal effectively with them. God already knows how you feel, so don't try to cover it up: "Until the Lord come, who both will bring to light the hidden things of darkness, and will make manifest the counsels of the hearts" (1 Cor. 4:5 KJV).

Bring your feelings out into the open where God can heal them and help you overcome them. Psalm 32:3 speaks of the futility of trying to keep them in: "When I kept silent, my bones grew old / Through my groaning all the day long" (NKJV). Then the psalmist goes on to say in verse 5: "I acknowledged my sin to You, / And my iniquity I have not hidden. / I said, 'I will confess my transgressions to the LORD,' / And You forgave the iniquity of my sin" (NKJV). God is able to do something about our hurts and sins if we will only acknowledge them. But if we don't acknowledge them, they will destroy us until we rot from the inside out.

Think before you speak. Look beyond your own hurts and see what is best for your child. Although you don't have to tell him every detail about the divorce, it's equally important not to hide everything from him. Children can learn amazing lessons from their parents' mistakes. But during your instructional time, make sure you don't go into all the glorious details of your ex-spouse's shortcomings. Doing so will cause more damage than good.

When you are trying to explain certain actions of your ex to your children, let your words be seasoned with grace. Keep in mind that you are speaking about the parent of your children and be merciful. Remember that we all have made mistakes—so be ready to share about some of your own mistakes too.

Situations involving the sexual or physical abuse of your child by your ex-spouse require even more care. For your child's protection, you or the court may place certain limits on their time together. When discussing the reasons for those limits, try to be sensitive to the conflicting emotions your son or daughter will be feeling. No matter how bad a parent your ex may be, he or she is still your child's mom or dad. Leave an open door for your child to talk about his feelings. Remember that denial is not the answer.

Sit him down and explain to him that Mom or Dad has a problem and needs to change. Make sure he understands that what happened was not his fault. And be careful not to continually reopen the wound once it starts to heal. Working this through without dragging everyone through the mud requires a real sensitivity to the Holy Spirit on your part. You want to help your child work through his emotions to the point of forgiveness and healing. Your goal is the healing of your child and not the punishment of your ex-husband or ex-wife. Keep this in mind whenever you need to discuss the situation with him.

If you've remarried or are planning to, don't compare your ex to the stepparent. It will automatically breed resentment in your children toward the new parent. Nothing can take the place of a mom or dad in a child's heart. Trying to build up the stepparent by tearing down your ex will only be counterproductive and make acceptance of a stepparent more difficult.

The words you say about your ex-spouse carry weight. Let those words carry healing rather than destruction. Make the building up of your children your aim. If you focus on the negative about your ex-husband or ex-wife, you will put your children in the middle of two people they love. On the other hand, if you put bitterness aside and seek to honor the relationship between your children and their other parent, your children and you will both be winners.

Affirmation: *I speak only those things about my ex-spouse that are edifying and encouraging to my children. Refusing to give place to bitterness, I trust God to heal me of the wounds and hurts inflicted through the divorce. I honor the relationship between parent and child and do not seek to separate my child's affections from his other parent. God is turning my scars into stars and my trials into testimonies.*

Affirmation Scriptures:
Hebrews 12:15; Romans 12:21; Matthew 5:44; and 1 Corinthians 4:5.

56

Dealing with Stepchildren

WITH CLOSE to 50 percent of Christian families breaking up through divorce, many born-again believers are finding themselves in second marriages dealing with ready-made families. Sadly, the divorce rate for second marriages is even higher than that of first-time marriages—especially if children are involved. Many people, even Christians, don't know how to handle stepchildren. This failure to establish a healthy relationship with the children of your new spouse can be disastrous, as reflected by the divorce rate for second marriages. Dealing with stepchildren can be an adventure, frustrating and rewarding all at the same time!

Parents involved in a second marriage should exercise special understanding for what their own children may be experiencing. It has been said that a child can understand the death of a parent easier than he can deal with a divorce. Often this is true because of the sense of betrayal that accompanies the breakup of a family. Whether or not the children are a source of conflict, they may still feel let down or even responsible to a certain degree. The remarriage of their parent adds a finality to the divorce that can be hard for them to accept.

As the child of a broken home, I personally experienced the challenges involved in merging two separate families into one. When I was a teenager, my father remarried and brought a brand-new person (or should I say persons) into my life. I found myself thrust into a situation with new brothers and sisters not of my own choosing. I don't think I would have picked them as friends, and I am quite sure they would not have picked me. In retrospect, my dad was not the best stepfather, and my stepmother was not the perfect new mom, either. Nevertheless, we were stuck together. So we decided to make the best of it. We were going to get along, period. And most of the time, we did.

Because of the divorce, much insecurity developed between the parents and the children in the family. My stepmother and I were constantly vying for my father's attention. We felt as if we were in competition with each other. Then one night, after I finally realized what was going on, my stepmother and I sat down and agreed that my dad had enough love for both of us. We concluded that we could share him and not compete for his attention.

Some children, however, may never seem to understand this fact. They continue to see the stepparent as a direct descendant of Attila the Hun. They envision him dragging his knuckles on the ground, carrying a huge club, and locking them in their rooms with only minor excursions out to perform slave labor tasks.

You can put to rest this misconception of the heartless and threatening stepparent and pave the way for a healthy relationship with your spouse's children. The following things will help you to draw your stepchildren to you and not to push them away.

Number one, be understanding. You will be amazed at the difference this will make in your relationship with your stepchildren. Put yourself in their shoes and try looking at the situation from their perspective. It will cause you to be a lot more tolerant. Recognize that this is a big adjustment for them. Not only are they adjusting to the fact that they will never again live in a home where both of their parents reside, but they are also working through the challenges of accepting a new parent and/or siblings into their inner circle.

Number two, never speak badly about the other parent of your stepchildren. You may hear that your spouse's ex is saying all sorts of terrible things about you or your spouse, but you can't let yourself respond in kind. It is not going to do you any good to rip into them.

Remember that your spouse's ex is still their mom or dad. It will only drive a wedge between you and your stepchildren if you criticize their biological parent and force them to choose between the two of you. Nine times out of ten, they will choose their biological parent.

Number three, don't be the "heavy." You will have to come to them as a friend and not as an iron-fisted parent—at least until you've proved to them that you are *for* them and not *against* them. One of the most common mistakes new stepparents make is to move immediately into the role of disciplinarian before having a chance to form good, solid relationships with their stepchildren. Discipline without relationship can lead to rebellion. Now, I am not advocating that you let your stepchildren run wild. Rather, I am encouraging you to ease into the role, taking the time to gain the respect and trust of your stepchildren. Once you have gained their confidence, they will be much more likely to respond positively to any discipline you may administer.

Number four, show affection. Children need to know that you care about them. A squeeze of the hand, a hug, or a pat on the back can go a long way in communicating love and concern. Studies have shown that babies need to be physically touched in order to thrive. Young children desire to be held and hugged. This need for physical affection does not cease to exist as children grow up. Although teenagers may not always feel as comfortable with overt demonstrations of affection, they still need a caring touch whether they admit it or not. Be sensitive to the specific needs of each child in this area; some children may be more comfortable with certain types of affection than they are with others.

Number five, spend time with them. Take time to get to know who they really are, what they feel and think. Try taking them out for ice cream or on walks with just the two of you. Find out what they like to do and do it with them. Invest in your relationship and expect your investment to pay off.

Forming a healthy relationship with your stepchildren is key to maintaining a happy home and strengthening your new marriage.

Take the time to get to know them and to earn their trust and respect. Reach out in ways that they can receive and show them that you really care. Keep in mind that they are making many new adjustments before you react hastily to things they do that upset you. And keep the communication lines open. Listen to their concerns and do not react before you know the whole story: "Wherefore, my beloved brethren, let every man be swift to hear, slow to speak, slow to wrath: For the wrath of man worketh not the righteousness of God" (James 1:19–20 KJV).

Most of all, seek to be a blessing to them. God has placed you as a steward over your stepchildren, to protect them and to help them grow up to be successful, godly, and well adjusted. In other words, love them deeply and sincerely from the heart.

Affirmation: *I thank You, Lord, for the blessing that my stepchildren are to me. I am excited about the opportunity You have given me to get to know them and be a part of their lives. Help them through the many adjustments they are making by becoming part of a new family. I praise You that they trust and respect me and respond well to discipline because they are secure in the fact that I love them and want the best for them.*

Affirmation Scriptures:
Galatians 5:22–23; John 17:23; and Philippians 4:6–7.

57

Absentee Parenting

WITHOUT QUESTION, absentee parenting is becoming increasingly prevalent in our society during this new millennium. More parents are on the road with their jobs now than ever before, sometimes returning home only for weekends and holidays. Someone once asked me whether it was possible for a teenager to function in that kind of an environment. Although teenagers can survive in almost any environment, the aim is not just surviving—we want to see them thriving. I have a friend with only one arm, and he tells me that although he gets by with one arm pretty well, it would be easier with two. Your teenager can get by with only one parent or guardian at home, but I can assure you that it is a whole lot easier with two.

Before we relocated to Oklahoma from Florida, I had to spend every Sunday night through Friday afternoon in Tulsa. Then I would fly back to Florida and spend Friday night through Sunday afternoon with my family. My wife and son didn't get to see me for five whole days each week. When I came home, I had to purpose in my heart that the weekend was not my own. It belonged to my family. I could be dog tired or craving a game of golf with the guys or a fishing trip with my friends, but I knew that because I was gone so much, there was no way I could do it. My family needed me. I decided that I was going to enjoy my time with my family instead of walking around the house moping with my bottom lip out because I did not have any time for me.

Then there was the challenge of fitting back into the normal flow of activity in the household. While I was gone, my wife developed her own system of doing things during the week. When I came home on the weekends, I just seemed to mess it all up. I had to be very sensitive to the challenges posed by that and try to look at the situation from her perspective rather than from mine alone. I found out that I could talk about God first, family second, and job third, but "*Man, this is where the rubber meets the road!*"

Although it was tough being gone from my family for so long, we still made it through those weeks of transition. But, wow, was it a stretch for us all! Making it through those tough times took dedication and understanding on the part of every member of the family.

If you are an absentee parent because you travel with your job or because you are divorced, you can still be a successful parent. However, it will require selflessness and effort on your part. If you will put the following things into practice, it will help you make the best out of a tough situation.

First, be considerate. In Romans 12:10, God's Word tells us to honor one another above ourselves. You will probably need to remind yourself continually of this exhortation, because the tendency is to be selfish, especially when we are tired. Don't make the mistake of coming home from a trip and barking orders at your family. Instead, stop to think about their needs and find out what you can do for them. Look for ways to make their lives easier instead of looking to have them cater to your needs. You may end up taking your children to buy some new clothes or helping them with their math when all you feel like doing is crashing on the couch.

If you spend time away from your children because you are divorced and do not have full custody of them, you will probably have to work even harder to meet their special needs. Children from a broken home often miss out on the little things that children from two-parent families take for granted—like baking cookies or cupcakes to take to their classmates at school or going on family camping trips and outings. The custodial parent is too busy trying to make ends meet to take care of some of those extras. That is where the noncustodial parent can help by picking up the slack. Again, it all comes back to putting others first.

Second, watch how you spend your time. Knowing the propensity of human nature to slip into that vegetative state called sloth, God instructs us to redeem the time because the days are evil (see Eph. 5:16). You may want to sit in front of the television and watch time slip by, but your weekend with your family will be gone before you know it. Your children need to know that you realize they're alive. If all you do when you come home is watch TV, read the paper, or go out with your friends, you will effectively send your family a big red signal that they are not as important to you. To avoid this, you may even want to limit yourself to a certain amount of television when you are home so that you don't unconsciously let it take over your time with your family.

Third, guard your attitude. Being happy is a choice, not an event dependent on circumstances. It's a choice that will give you strength to make it through this tough time (see Neh. 8:10). We all have a greater tendency to get cranky and whiny when we are tired. And nothing can make a person quite so tired as traveling on a regular basis. When the noise and activity levels in the house begin to rise, take an attitude check and count to ten before reacting. Remember that you can do all things through Christ who strengthens you (see Phil. 4:13).

Finally, do something fun with your kids. Memories are made of this stuff. A famous lecturer used to tell audiences about the one event that changed his life—the day his father took him fishing. When comparing the journal entries of the father to those made by the son on that day, biographers of this famous lecturer were amazed to see the difference in view. The son had written more than five pages about the day he went fishing with his dad. The father's entry, on the other hand, read: "Went fishing with son, day wasted." Some things may not seem that monumental to you, but they could be life changing to your family. Take your kids out to dinner or do something fun that promotes communication between you. One thing that can be especially great is a family game-night every week where you play board (or other) games together.

Absentee moms and dads can still be great parents; it just takes a little more effort and selflessness on their parts. When trying to make the most of the times you do have together with your children, remember to keep Romans 12:10 as the rule of thumb. Put yourself in their places and try to understand their needs. Especially in situations caused by a divorce, the effort you make will deeply impact your relationship with your children, bringing healing and restoration. Although you may be tired from traveling or from working all week, it will be well worth it.

Affirmation: *Thank You, Lord, for helping me to see the needs of my family so that I can more effectively minister to those needs. I make a conscious effort to subdue my selfish wishes, to bless my children rather than seek to be blessed. I can do all things through Christ who strengthens me.*

Affirmation Scriptures:
Romans 12:10; Philippians 4:13; and James 1:19.

58

How to Keep a Happy Home

DURING MY YEARS in ministry, I have had so many people approach me and say, "I just want to be happy like you. I sure wish God would give me some of the joy you have." The exciting thing is that anyone can have that kind of joy. One of the greatest revelations I have ever received is to understand that joy is a choice. If we want to live a life filled with gladness, we have to make a decision to be joyful. It does not happen by accident. We choose to be happy, and we choose to have a happy family. After we make that decision, we must stick with it. If you as a parent choose to walk in joy, your attitude and leadership will affect the attitudes of the rest of the family. Just remember that it has to start with you.

On the average, we have about thirty things happen to us every day that can rob us of our joy. This is especially true where other people are involved. During those times, we need to remember that God has placed joy as a fruit in our spirits. It's up to us to decide not to let anything or anyone cause that fruit to go sour.

One of the main reasons people lose their joy is that they mistakenly think the tough time will never end; they feel as if it will last the rest of their lives. But that is not true. We need to realize that our trials are only going to last for a little while. In fact, God's Word tells us that we need to rejoice because we are guarded by our faith although for "a little while" we might suffer trials (1 Peter 1:6 NKJV). Thus, the Bible assures us that there will be an end to our suffering. It will not last forever.

The knowledge that our trials will only last a short time gives us an excellent reason to rejoice in the middle of them. Our breakthrough is coming. We cannot turn loose of our faith or our joy now. We have a promise that tells us, "Many are the afflictions of the righteous, / But the LORD delivers him out of them all" (Ps. 34:19 NKJV). We need to look up, for our "redemption draweth nigh" (Luke 21:28 KJV).

Another thing that will help you keep your joy is to look for something humorous in the middle of your trial no matter how tough it may be. You can keep your sense of humor even in the middle of great difficulty. I have experienced days when so many things went wrong that I just started to laugh. I thought, *Wow, this is so bad, it's funny.* We can laugh our way through the tough times, or we can cry our way through them. Either way, we are still going to go through them. I will tell you this, however: It's a whole lot easier to laugh!

Remember that the joy of the Lord is your strength (see Neh. 8:10). Don't let the enemy steal your strength. Hang on to it. Holding on to the joy of the Lord will give you the ability to keep going even when you can't see the end. In Proverbs we are told, "The spirit of a man will sustain him in sickness, / But who can bear a broken spirit?" (Prov. 18:14 NKJV). If you let go of your joy, you will develop a wounded spirit. If you keep your joy, your spirit will sustain you through your infirmity or other trial.

Keep a song in your heart. The happiest people I have ever met are people who always have a song in their hearts. God's Word tells the barren woman to sing (see Isa. 54:1). You may not have given birth to your breakthrough yet, but you can still sing praises to God. Your children may be going through tough times; the enemy may be pounding on your marriage. But go ahead and sing, right in the middle of this attack.

When you do sing praises to the Lord in the middle of a trial, something supernatural begins to happen. In fact, the Bible says that it will "silence the enemy and the avenger" (Ps. 8:2 NKJV). It will also put the enemy to flight. When King Jehoshaphat went out to battle against the enemy, he put singers at the front of the army to praise the Lord. The Word says that as they went before the people singing and praising God, the Lord set ambushes for the enemy and defeated them (see 2 Chron. 20:21–22). God did their fighting for them and put the enemy to flight.

Another thing that will help you remain joyful under trial is to keep your focus on the good and not on the bad. Stay positive. If someone is going to blow it, this is usually where he or she will mess up. On what kind of things do you meditate? If you can get a grip on your thought life and focus on the positive rather than the negative, you will see the power of God released in your life:

> Finally, brethren, whatever things are true, whatever things are noble, whatever things are just, whatever things are pure, whatever things are lovely, whatever things are of good report, if there is any virtue and if there is anything praiseworthy—meditate on these things. (Phil. 4:8 NKJV)

Make a choice to be happy and to keep your home happy. Do not let your troubles get you down. Instead, put your troubles where they belong—under your feet. Focus on the promises of God and remember that your trial is only for a season. It will not last forever. So lift your voice and praise God, because deliverance is coming!

Affirmation: *I rejoice in the Lord even in the midst of difficulty. I lift my voice in praise to Him because I know that He will surely deliver me out of my affliction. Because I know that He is faithful, I never let anything steal my joy from me. I make a choice to be happy and to lead my family into a life of happiness too.*

Affirmation Scriptures:
Philippians 4:8; Psalm 106:3; and Nehemiah 8:10.

59

Helping Your Teen Adjust to a Move

CHANGE CAN BE HARD on anyone, especially teenagers. Adolescents are already dealing with many changes due to increased hormone levels, physical growth, and emotional development. When you add other variables, it can make them feel overloaded and insecure. Home is typically considered a teen's most dependable "safe place." When everything else in their lives seems to be in transition, this is the one constant on which they depend. And if that changes too, it can be a major crisis for them.

"Amanda" had just finished her junior year in high school when her mother was called to interview for a position with an out-of-state ministry. This job appeared to be a tremendous opportunity for her mom, both to work in ministry and for promotion. All the way around, it looked good. When Amanda and her mom flew down for the interview, her mom fell in love with the place. Although Amanda was also excited about the opportunity, she suddenly broke down in tears at the prospect of moving. She was tied into her school, her friends, and church, and could not imagine missing her senior year there. She just was not prepared to relocate, no matter how good the opportunity looked.

Whenever a family relocates to a new city or area, the parents should actively seek to make the transition as easy as possible. With the exception of the family unit, everything else in their teenager's life has changed. And sometimes even that changes, if the move is due to a divorce.

Family ties become increasingly important to children in times like these. One way you can help prepare your children is to strengthen the bonds between members of the family ahead of time. Spend more time together and plan special family outings. Do things that facilitate a sense of camaraderie. The stronger the ties, the more secure your teen will be in moving to a new location because her closest friends—parents and siblings—will be moving with her.

Focus on the new and exciting adventures to come. Through successful PR work, parents can foster expectation rather than regret. Teens should be encouraged to focus on the new opportunities ahead. Talk about the new places they will see and experience. Check out the local attractions to discover what type of recreation is available; plan activities like swimming, boating, hiking, playing miniature golf, or going to an amusement park. Whatever the terrain, new and exciting things exist for your children to see and do. This move is only part of the great adventure God has for them. God has so much more in store for us than we can possibly leave behind:

> So Jesus answered and said, "Assuredly, I say to you, there is no one who has left house or brothers or sisters or father or mother or wife or children or lands, for My sake and the gospel's, who shall not receive a hundredfold now in this time—houses and brothers and sisters and mothers and children and lands, with persecutions—and in the age to come, eternal life." (Mark 10:29–30 NKJV)

Actively seek your teen's input on decisions relating to where you will live. Take your family with you to help pick out your new home and encourage them to start planning the decor for their new bedrooms. You need to give your teenager her own space—engendering a feeling of control and possession in at least one area of her life. When everything else seems to be spinning out of her control, allowing her to help choose your new house or to decorate her room will give her a sense of ownership in her life. It will also make her feel that she is part of the decision-making process, and that will help her to buy into the move.

Amazingly enough, God seeks the input of His children. Our heavenly Father longs for us to talk things over with Him, to share our feelings and thoughts with Him: "Come now, and let us reason together" (Isa. 1:18 NKJV). We should follow His example and seek out our children's feelings and ideas concerning potential changes.

Make as few other changes as possible. Wait until your family has had the chance to settle in and adjust to the move. Try not to alter the furniture, get rid of the family pet, or do anything else new around the house for a while. This will add stability and security to the lives of your children while they experience so much transition in other areas. Remember that they are making new friends, saying good-bye to old ones, and adjusting to new schools with new teachers and students. Even their church is unfamiliar to them.

Locate a new church home. Having a church family is so important. Although cultural differences may exist, true believers are still family wherever you go. We worship the same God and follow the same Book of ethics. Even in the jungles of a faraway country, we can find a group of believers to call family. And, as the Word says, we are all part of the same household: "Therefore, as we have opportunity, let us do good to all, especially to those who are of the household of faith" (Gal. 6:10 NKJV).

Make friends with families who have children the same age as yours. This is a great way to help your children develop friendships with other kids. Plan fun excursions that facilitate the development of good relationships among the children of the two families. Whenever the two families get together, your kids will have ready-made friends to play with.

Get your children involved in local sports or other extracurricular activities. Sports teams and other group activities provide your teen with an excellent opportunity to make new friends and quickly gain a sense of belonging. Try coaching their soccer or baseball team. The more involved you are, the better it will be for them.

Reach out to your new neighbors; don't wait for them to come to you. The sooner you develop a rapport with those you live near, the sooner you will feel at home in your new house. It can also help your children get to know other kids in the neighborhood and form new friendships.

Encourage your children to talk to you about any negative feelings they may have concerning the move. Keep the communication lines open—your kids need to be able to talk through any feelings of insecurity or sorrow they might have from relocating. If they believe they have an open door to talk with you, they will be less likely to turn inward or find solace elsewhere. Just knowing that you care enough to listen may be all the assurance they need.

Most of all, be there for them. Whether it is to give them a sounding board for their questions and concerns or to drive them to a new friend's house, be accessible. Chauffeur them places with their new friends and facilitate fun activities. Whatever they do, they will need your support.

Approaching your upcoming move from a positive standpoint can make the transition easier for every member of your family. Be sensitive to their feelings and open to their input. By focusing on the opportunities ahead and including them in the decision-making process, you will help them look forward to the move and expect good things from God. And remember to walk in love; it never fails!

Affirmation: *My children are excited about our upcoming move. They expect You to meet their need for friends, a new school, and a good church. We seek to make this move free from stress and actively desire the input of our children on major decisions such as locating a new church, finding a* *new home, and decorating their rooms. We buy into the move as a family and take full advantage of all the new opportunities it affords us. Thank You, Lord, for making this transition easy for all of us.*

Affirmation Scriptures:
Jeremiah 29:11; Mark 10:29–30; and Romans 8:38–39.

60

Dealing with a Death in the Family

WE ALL must face death at some point in our lives. Whether it is the death of a loved one or an acquaintance, or even our own deaths, eventually we will encounter it. Death is never easy, even for adults, but it can be especially hard on a teenager. Teens are often so idealistic that they fail to include death in the mix of life. When anyone or anything—from a family member or a close friend to the family pet—dies, it can be quite traumatic.

When I was fifteen, my grandmother passed away. She was over sixty years old and had multiple sclerosis. Although she was confined to a wheelchair for most of my childhood (eventually becoming bedridden), I was still unprepared for her death. It had a profound effect on me. I was not living for the Lord at that point in my life and really didn't want to have anything to do with Him.

When she died, a penetrating revelation hit me. I realized that everyone was going to die eventually, and I began to ask myself what I was doing with my own life. As the Scripture says, "It is appointed for men to die once, but after this the judgment" (Heb. 9:27 NKJV). This revelation went straight to my heart, and I can point to this moment as the beginning of my serious search for purpose in life and of my personal quest for a relationship with God through Jesus Christ.

Through working with young people, I have counseled many teens who have lost parents or siblings to a premature death. One thing I have noticed is that teens have a tendency to struggle with guilt. They ask themselves, "What if I had done *this* or *that?* My loved one might still be alive today." In one way or another, they take upon themselves the blame for their loved one's death. Although God is a giver of life rather than death, some teens even blame God for the death of the person they love.

If your teen has recently experienced the death of someone close to him, he will need your help to get through his grief and on to the healing process. The following are some suggestions for parents to help their teens try to make the best out of a difficult situation.

Give credit to whom credit is due. Many people have a tendency to blame God for things the enemy does, especially when it comes to the death of someone close to them. Introduced into the world through the fall of man, death was never a part of God's original plan: "Therefore, just as through one man sin entered the world, and death through sin, and thus death spread to all men, because all sinned" (Rom. 5:12 NKJV).

The Scripture makes it clear that Jesus healed people "oppressed by the *devil*," *not* people who were oppressed by *God* (Acts 10:38 NKJV, emphasis mine). God is not the source of oppression. Rather, Jesus is our Healer, and the devil is the oppressor. Understanding this principle will help your teenager see that God is a loving God. It will help him realize that God is for him, not against him.

Remember that God is a God of comfort. In the midst of tough times, God is faithful to pour out His comfort on us. The fact is that He is going to give us so much comfort that we will even be able to help others:

Blessed be God, even the Father of our Lord Jesus Christ, the Father of mercies, and the God of all comfort; who comforteth us in all our tribulation, that we may be able to comfort them which are in any trouble, by the comfort wherewith we ourselves are comforted of God. (2 Cor. 1:3–4 KJV)

Over the years, I have spoken with numerous people who have gone through tragic experiences. They say that while they were walking through the crisis they felt as if they were in a dream. Rather than intense sorrow, they often felt numb. I truly believe that this lack of feeling during such tragedies is a grace from God (the comfort of the Holy Spirit) to help them make it through a very traumatic time without being overwhelmed by grief.

We are not alone. One of the primary tools the enemy uses is to try to convince us that no one else understands what we are going through. Feelings like this bring about a sense of isolation and detachment from other people. The good news is that other people have already gone through it and have overcome. That is why God's Word tells us to take a stand against the enemy. We are to be strong in our faith, remembering that our Christian brothers and sisters all over the world are going through the same kind of suffering (1 Peter 5:9). Sometimes it helps to know that others have been through the same thing and have come out victoriously.

God will go beyond comfort and bring your teen into healing. Often we mistakenly believe that we will have to tolerate a particular hurt in our hearts for the rest of our lives. This is not true. God is the Healer of the brokenhearted. He repairs and mends our wounded parts; He does not leave us forever damaged.

It is important to realize that one of the major reasons for Jesus' coming and death on the cross was to "heal the brokenhearted" (Luke 4:18 NKJV). It is easy to be deceived when you are young, to think that you will feel pain for the rest of your life. In the Word, however, God indicates that our suffering is only for a season: "Though now for a season, if need be, ye are in heaviness" (1 Peter 1:6 KJV). That is King James language for, "These feelings will only last a little while."

Several years ago my father died of cancer. For the first few months after his death, every time I thought of him I remembered his last three months of life in bed. All I could see was my dad fading in and out of a coma while lying in bed with tubes coming out of his arm.

That picture of him suffering stayed in my mind for a while. However, as time went on, I began to recall the good times instead. I remembered the times he played catch with me in the yard, the camping trips we took, and the fun experiences we shared together. Now when someone mentions my father, or if I pick up something nostalgic that reminds me of him, I find myself smiling because of all the great times we had together. This happened with the passing of time. It is amazing how it truly does get easier as the years go by. God uses time to heal hurts in our hearts.

Share personal experiences of your own. When you talk to your teen about something that caused you pain and hurt and explain how you got over it, you are saying, "I understand how you feel." That makes a difference. It helps him to see that he, too, can make it. It also helps him realize that you have compassion for him because you have been through it too.

Touch him. So many barriers are broken down with a touch. When you touch or hug your child, you release major healing in his life. In the gospel of Mark, we see Jesus approached by a leper desiring Jesus to heal him (see Mark 1:40–42). In response, Jesus did something remarkable. He not only spoke to him, releasing healing virtue; He also touched him. I am sure that His touch took care of so much rejection, because through it, Jesus said, "I accept you; I love you. You mean so much to Me."

When a teenager has experienced some sort of tragedy in his life, like losing a loved one, sometimes all he needs is to have you hold him while he cries. Do not pull away first; wait for him to pull away when he is ready. That hug might last several minutes or maybe even longer, but don't rush it. Stay there for as long as he needs you.

There is more to life than living here on earth. Death is just as much a part of life as birth. It is a graduation and promotion for all those who are saved, moving from one realm of glory into another. This is why Paul said that he was torn between two desires when it came to choosing between living and dying: "I'm torn between two desires: Sometimes I want to live, and sometimes I long to go and be with Christ. That would be far better for me" (Phil. 1:23 NLT).

We do not sorrow as the world does because we have hope (see 1 Thess. 4:13). The Bible assures us that God has good plans for us, plans to give us a future and a hope (see Jer. 29:11). And that future includes spending eternity in glory with our beloved Lord and Savior.

Affirmation: *Thank You, Lord, for helping my teenager to get through grief and into healing. You are an ever-present comfort to him, and he is able to help others with the comfort he has received. Thank You for using this encounter with death to prompt him to examine his own life and make godly and wise decisions. My teenager is comfortable sharing his feelings of grief with me and receives comfort from my personal experiences of overcoming grief. He is an overcomer!*

Affirmation Scriptures:
2 Corinthians 1:3–4; 1 Thessalonians 4:13–14; Jeremiah 29:11; and Psalm 25:4–5.

61

Dealing with Financial Pressure

PURSUIT OF the great American dream has buried many families under an enormous mountain of debt. We want a new car or find a sale we just can't seem to resist. If we don't have the finances ourselves, we run to the banker for his help. The problem is that debt does not help. In the end, it enslaves and imprisons all who get entangled in its web. We may have a new car or a new dress, but we also have a new monthly bill to pay. And if we miss too many monthly payments, the bank can come and take everything we have.

Our vision to finance a global harvest of souls has often been forced to give way to ever-increasing stacks of debt. But it's not only the American family that is enslaved to debt. Churches and ministries also have buried themselves so much under this financial mountain that the focal point of the service centers upon the offering rather than on the worship or the message.

Few things stifle the potency of people and their ministries more than debt. It keeps people chained to lack. Debt keeps you poor, and no one listens to a poor man:

This wisdom I have also seen under the sun, and it seemed great to me: There was a little city with few men in it; and a great king came against it, besieged it, and built great snares around it. Now there was found in it a poor wise man, and he by his wisdom delivered the city. Yet no one remembered that same poor man. Then I said:

"Wisdom is better than strength.
Nevertheless the poor man's wisdom is despised,
And his words are not heard." (Eccl. 9:13–16 NKJV)

It has caused us to relinquish the abundance with which God desires to bless us. And we are not able to bless others because we ourselves are in need of so much help. Debt and credit, along with interest payments, have enslaved us, keeping us in the prison of financial lack.

When financial pressure hits a family, it not only causes stress between husband and wife; it affects the children as well. The whole family begins to feel the impact as the belt tightens and irritability increases. The peace of the home is compromised because we don't have the self-control to wait until we can pay for our purchases in cash.

To help break this cycle of family debt, parents need to train their children to handle their finances wisely. Don't wait until your children are teenagers before you begin to teach these important principles. Start while they are young. If parents fail to instruct their children on fiscal responsibility, their children will learn from those who do not have their best interests at heart. They will learn from the bank or the credit card company. But if they learn from you instead of the lending institution, the lessons will go easier and be more profitable for them.

"Train up a child in the way he should go, / And when he is old he will not depart from it. / The rich rules over the poor, / And the borrower is servant to the lender" (Prov. 22:6–7 NKJV). These two verses discuss a parent's obligation to train up his child properly and seek to address the negative consequences of debt. If we are to train our children properly, we cannot fail to include such important financial information. We don't want our kids to be ruled by the bank or the credit card company.

The sad thing is that often our example is completely opposite to the principles we desire to impart. We raise our children in a house with a thirty-year mortgage attached to it and drive them to school in a car purchased on a five-year note. They sleep on financed beds and study with financed encyclopedias. We buy clothes with credit cards and wash them in a machine purchased on a revolving charge account. When they turn eighteen, we take them to a bank and co-sign on their first loan, thus launching them into their own ocean of red ink. Our actions speak so loudly that our children are unable to hear our words telling them to stay out of debt.

If we teach our children God's principles of finance through both our words and our actions, the chains of debt can be broken. We can train our sons and our daughters to believe God and practice biblical principles. They need to know that money does not come from Santa Claus, the Easter Bunny, or the Tooth Fairy; it comes through faith in God. It is God who gives us the "power to get wealth" (Deut. 8:18 NKJV).

Many people seem to be uncomfortable talking about money, and yet the Bible is full of verses dealing specifically with this subject. In the New Testament alone, there are more than two hundred verses dealing with money. When we combine the Old and New Testaments, that number increases to more than two thousand verses. Sixteen of the parables in the Word deal with money. Amazingly, only five hundred verses speak about prayer, while another five hundred address the subject of faith. Evidently, God wants to talk about money even if no one else does!

If you are currently debt free, I have one thing to say: Stay out of it. Keep living within your budget and believe God for those things that go beyond it. If you are currently struggling to pay off some loans or credit cards, however, and there does not seem to be enough money to go around, I would encourage you to do the following.

First, trust God with your finances. The primary reason we become stressed when finances are tight is that we fail to trust God to meet those needs we can't meet ourselves. We need to remember that God is our heavenly Father. Just as we desire to provide for all of our children's needs, so does God desire to provide for ours. The difference between God and us is that God is always able to provide for whatever we need. His resources are unlimited. God wants us to seek Him first; He will take care of the rest:

> Therefore do not worry, saying, "What shall we eat?" or "What shall we drink?" or "What shall we wear?" For after all these things the Gentiles seek. For your heavenly Father knows that you need all these things. But seek first the kingdom of God and His righteousness, and all these things shall be added to you. (Matt. 6:31–33 NKJV)

Second, expect a miracle. I know a couple who went through a time where they learned to trust God with their finances in a miraculous way. The husband had been severely injured in an accident and was essentially bedridden and unable to work. To complicate things, they had just moved to a new area where employment in the wife's profession was practically nonexistent. They had a new baby and two other children. The only work the wife could find was a part-time job teaching English at a Christian school for around six hundred dollars a month, just enough to cover their rent. Their situation really appeared hopeless.

When you only have six hundred dollars a month to cover the needs of a family of five, the money gets used up pretty quickly. It was not long before they were down to their last dollar. When the offering was passed around at church, the wife put that dollar in the bucket, naming her harvest to God: "God, I sow this seed of faith for money to pay our rent. I choose to believe You no matter how bad it looks. I expect a miracle." Her husband was also speaking to God about their need, claiming his harvest from the sowing of "their widow's mite" (see Luke 21:1–4). Together, she and her husband agreed in faith that God would provide.

It took only two weeks for them to receive the answer to their prayer. A friend who was a Catholic priest called up and offered to pay their rent indefinitely. That priest paid their rent for a year and a half until they were back on their feet again. God had worked a miracle on their behalf, taking what seemed to be an insignificant amount of money (one dollar) and multiplying it over and over again.

Third, put yourself on a budget. I like John Osteen's advice: Sit on the floor until you can afford a box. Don't purchase items for which you have no money. Wait until you can fit the purchase into the budget. Then you can buy it without regret, without stress, and without a new monthly payment.

Next, obey the principles of seedtime and harvest. Give and expect to reap a harvest. A popular doctrine today claims that God does not prosper people because He can't trust them with money. While there is an element of truth to the fact that not everyone can be trusted with money, lack on the part of the people of God cannot automatically be associated with it. Statements like this throw the whole responsibility for prosperity back on God. It assumes that God has failed to trust His people and ignores the failure of many to plant seed through giving.

Many times our lack of prosperity is because we have not done what God has commanded in His Word. We have not fulfilled our end of the covenant; we have not given Him the seed to multiply. It would be a crazy farmer indeed who believed he could raise an entire crop of wheat without planting any seed. "Seedtime and harvest" is a God-ordained principle, and "sowing and reaping" is His outline for financial success. Putting these principles into practice is an essential prerequisite to financial abundance.

Fifth, confess abundance and keep your eyes on the Giver. We are bound by the words of our mouths. If we continually complain about our financial difficulty, we will reap more hardship. If we want abundance, we must speak abundance:

So Jesus answered and said to them, "Assuredly, I say to you, if you have faith and do not doubt, you will not only do what was done to the fig tree, but also if you say to this mountain, 'Be removed and be cast into the sea,' it will be done." (Matt. 21:21 NKJV)

Keep the words of your mouth going in the direction you want to head. Remember that speaking negative words constantly can erode your faith and influence your attitude. Keep your eyes on Jesus and trust Him to provide for your needs.

Finally, check your attitude to ensure that you are not communicating stress to the rest of the family. Because financial pressure can affect every member of the household, it's important to check up constantly on our attitudes. Guard against communicating concern and fear to your children and spouse. It's all too easy to become irritable and snap at our loved ones because we are feeling the pressure of finances. Try to be aware so that you can avoid complicating your situation with fighting and bickering in the home.

Affirmation: *I am a believer and not a doubter. I am a giver and a receiver. God meets all of my needs because I seek Him first. I put into practice the principle of sowing and reaping and receive an abundant harvest of finances as I give in faith to God. I expect a miracle and trust God to bring it to pass. Worry and concern are far from me because I trust God to take care of my family and me. Our home remains peaceful and free from the stress of financial pressure.*

Affirmation Scriptures:
Matthew 6:31–33; Psalm 23:1; Philippians 4:19;
and Hebrews 4:16.

62

Teaching Your Teenager About Faith

FAITH IS A LEGACY that can be passed from one generation to the next. We are creating tomorrow's leaders out of our children today. The apostle Paul referred to this handing down of faith from parent to child in his second letter to Timothy: "I know that you sincerely trust the Lord, for you have the faith of your mother, Eunice, and your grandmother, Lois" (2 Tim. 1:5 NLT).

As parents, we have a responsibility to train our children in the principles of faith. This accountability encompasses more than just their salvation experience. It also Includes training them up in a lifestyle of faith. It means that we are to prepare our children to meet life's challenges with the unwavering conviction that God always keeps His promises and never breaks His word. He is faithful to perform His word even when circumstances look the darkest.

Faith is the foundation of our relationship with God and the vehicle of our salvation. We are delivered by faith; we are healed by faith. When we are old, we pass from this world to the next by faith. Without it, we can never hope to please God (see Heb. 11:6). It is eternal and powerful, able to move mountains through the spoken word (see Mark 11:23).

Faith can move the hearts of sinners to repentance. An evangelist friend of mine prepared for the first sermon he ever preached by praying and fasting for a week. The night that he preached, he claimed fifteen souls for God. No one had told him how small the response usually was in that church—that no more than five people at one time had ever responded to an altar call. He was just "too foolish" to know any better than to ask God and believe for such a harvest. In response to his faith, more than twenty hands went up for the altar call that evening.

Now you may not be an evangelist or a pastor, but if you are reading this book, there is an extremely good possibility that you are a parent. As a parent, you have a heritage of faith to pass on to your children.

Take time to instruct your teenager in the principles of God's Word. This is where a family altar comes in handy. Spend time in the Word with your child every day, teaching him the promises of God. Talking to him about the faithfulness of God will encourage him to believe God in his life as well. Be specific in your discussion of God's promises. Look up Scripture verses that apply to his specific needs and examine how he can believe God to meet those needs.

Teach him to speak the Word of God over his situation, to confess God's promises. We are bound by the words of our mouths. If we learn to speak faith-filled words, we will reap the harvest of faith. Our teens need to realize that their words have power, either for life or death (see Prov. 18:21). We need to encourage them to be aware of the words they speak, to help them control the type of seed they sow.

Help your teen learn to believe God for his personal needs and desires, to establish his own faith projects. If your son or daughter desires a new outfit or even a car, teach him to bring his request to God. By going to God first for his need, he will strengthen and increase his faith.

Brittany was a young girl who loved to buy presents for other people. One year at Christmas, she told her mother that she wanted fifty dollars to buy presents for all her family and friends. Instead of automatically funding her generosity, her mom encouraged her to talk to God about it, to make it her own personal faith project. Determined to see her desire come to pass, Brittany prayed and asked God for the money.

Soon after she prayed, she received fifteen dollars in the mail as a birthday gift from her aunt in Florida. The church she was attending had been teaching on the principles of sowing and reaping, so she decided to sow her birthday money as a seed of faith. The amazing thing is, she set a time limit on how long God had to answer her prayer—exactly two weeks. Happy to give to God, she sowed her seed in expectant faith. She was confident that God would come through for her. Two weeks to the day after she gave her offering, she received a check in the mail from someone for fifty dollars. God had answered her prayer within her specified time frame.

This young woman of faith had been learning the principles of sowing and reaping both from her parents and from her church. She was being taught specific promises on which she could rely. She had been instructed in the ways of faith.

Develop family faith projects. As a group, agree together for something to come to pass and persevere until you see it happen. I know a family who believed for a home together. At the time, they had just graduated from Bible college and were renting a house near the campus. Deciding to locate permanently in the area, they began to pray for a new home.

After praying for several weeks with seemingly little or no result, they decided to seek God's will in the matter together as a family. Joining hands, they asked God if indeed He wanted them to buy a home in that city. Their daughter and one of their sons confirmed that God wanted them to buy a house. The daughter even went one step further; she said that they would have a home within ten days.

Although at the time it seemed a rather impossible task, they agreed every night together in prayer for their new house. Within ten days, they had a signed contract for a beautiful home at a bargain-basement price. Their family faith project was now complete.

We not only teach our children faith through our words, we also teach them faith through what we do and how we live. Let your teen see the reality of the Word of God in your life. If your child gets sick, first go to God for his healing. Pray over him; lay hands on him and believe God. I am not saying that you should never take your child to the doctor, but I am saying that you should put your faith in God and not in the doctor or the medicine. Train him to stay in faith even if he has to take medication prescribed by a physician.

Pulpits across the land preach on the principles of faith. We believe we know all there is to know about faith and can quote the relevant verses by heart. But if we do not live our faith, we are like the people in Hebrews: "The word which they heard did not profit them, not being mixed with faith in those who heard it" (Heb. 4:2 NKJV). Hearing and knowing the Word of God is not enough. We must demonstrate our faith through acting on the Word.

When Jesus told Peter to come down out of the boat and walk on the water, Peter acted. He did not consider the circumstances or the consequences of his actions. He stepped out of the boat and became a "water walker."

Real faith is contagious. Demonstrate true faith in your life, through your words and through your actions. Dare to believe God and step out of your boat. Be a water walker, and when you look over your shoulder, you will see your teenager following you.

Affirmation: *Thank You, Lord, for helping me to impart a legacy of faith to my children. Through my words and through my actions, I demonstrate real faith to my teen. He understands and walks in the principles of faith.*

Affirmation Scriptures:
Hebrews 11:1, 6; Hebrews 6:10–12; and Mark 11:22–24.

63

Don't Give Up

I THINK MOST people will agree that raising kids in today's world can be an adventure. Violence, hatred, abortion, drug and alcohol abuse, and teen suicide seem to abound more than ever before. Even drive-by shootings are starting to have an all too familiar sound. Many believe that this generation has no hope, identity, or purpose. But that isn't true. The good news is that it is possible to live for God in any generation. Through our faith in Jesus Christ, we always have the victory: "For whatsoever is born of God overcometh the world: and this is the victory that overcometh the world, even our faith" (1 John 5:4 KJV).

In reality, we are living in the most exciting time ever. As the manifestation of the devil increases, so much more does the power of God: "But where sin abounded, grace did much more abound" (Rom. 5:20 KJV). With the preaching of the gospel, miracles are happening all over the world. Millions are coming to Christ, and people are being healed from every kind of infirmity and disease (including AIDS).

We all want our children to live right, act right, and make right choices. But if we expect our children to live this way, we need to examine ourselves to ensure that we are instilling the right things into our children. How will they learn unless we teach and guide them by our examples? The Bible says,

Do not be deceived: God cannot be mocked. A man reaps what he sows. The one who sows to please his sinful nature, from that nature will reap destruction; the one who sows to please the Spirit, from the Spirit will reap eternal life. (Gal. 6:7–8 NIV)

Sowing and reaping is a kingdom principle. If we want our children to follow God and serve Him, we must invest in their lives while they are young. Otherwise, we may discover that we have unconsciously let the school system dictate their standard of morality and TV sitcoms serve as their examples. We have to be good stewards of the gifts with which God has blessed us—our children. As parents, we can be a living example to our children, sowing the Word of God into their hearts through our actions and words.

I have a close friend who was blessed enough to grow up in a Christian home. Her parents hung Scripture verses on the walls and took their children to church twice a week. Whenever revival was going on at church, Kim and her family were there. At an early age, she remembers her mother (a Sunday school teacher) working on projects and preparing Bible lessons. Not only did her mom teach the kids at church, but she also set an example for Kim and her brother through her commitment to God and His work. Her father also took the time to invest in her life, tucking her into bed every night and praying with her.

Although Kim and her brother both went through a period where their commitment to Christ wavered, each of them eventually returned to God. By the time Kim had entered high school, she had realized that it was not enough for just her mom and dad to have a relationship with the Lord. She knew she had to develop her own. Kim decided to make her own stand for God.

Confessing the Word over her life, she believed God for favor and received it. She was voted homecoming princess, homecoming queen, and even senior class president. Determined to bring glory to God in all that she did, she became known among her classmates for her Christian witness. Whenever her friends were in trouble, they called upon Kim to pray. One of her friends was even healed of an incurable disease after they prayed together in the girls' bathroom at school. Eventually, her brother recommitted his life to the Lord and went on to attend a Christian university.

Kim's parents took the time to sow the Word of God into her heart while she was young. Now Kim and her husband, Mike, travel all over the world, preaching the gospel and holding crusades in Third World countries. More than six million people have come to Christ through their ministry. Acknowledging the impact her parents had on her life, she is quick to say, "I am where I am today because of what my parents instilled into my heart when I was still a little girl."

You can't make your children serve God, but you can sow the Word into their lives. Take time to invest spiritually in your children now. Remember that the Word of God is alive and effective. Even if your teen tries to run from God, he will not be able to escape from God's presence. And when it looks grim and dark, and you feel as if the devil has a hold on your child's life, remember this: "So is my word that goes out from my mouth: / It will not return to me empty, / but will accomplish what I desire / and achieve the purpose for which I sent It" (Isa. 55:11 NIV).

Maybe you have not been a Christian for very long and have lacked the knowledge of how to sow God into your children's lives. You may have teenagers who are rebelling against your authority and running from the Lord. I want to encourage you to start sowing the right thing into their lives now—sow the eternal Word of God! Take hold of God's promises and start speaking over them. The Bible says,

I tell you the truth, if anyone says to this mountain, "Go, throw yourself into the sea," and does not doubt in his heart but believes that what he says will happen, it will be done for him. Therefore I tell you, whatever you ask for in prayer, believe that you have received it, and it will be yours. (Mark 11:23–24 NIV)

It doesn't matter how bad it looks—God can turn it around for you! God is faithful to His Word, so don't give up. Have faith in the seed you have sown into the hearts of your children. The harvest will come; His Word guarantees it.

Affirmation: *I rejoice in the opportunity to sow spiritual seed into the lives of my children. That seed is growing and growing, influencing them to follow God and serve Him with all of their hearts. The Word that I speak over my children does not return void. It instructs and trains them in the ways of God. Thank You, Lord, for godly children who love You and serve You with all their hearts and who walk in faith and the victory of Christ!*

Affirmation Scriptures:
Isaiah 55:11; Jeremiah 29:11; and Ephesians 3:20.

Notes

Chapter 2

1. Ken Anderson, Professor of Philosophy, Oxford College, Emery University.

Chapter 3

1. Webster's Collegiate Dictionary, 10th ed., s.v. "magnify."

Chapter 15

1. Albert Schweitzer in "Quotable Quotes," *Reader's Digest* (Pleasantville: Reader's Digest, 1997), .

Chapter 16

1. Glenn T. Stanton, "Twice as Strong: Two Parents–One Healthy Child," (Focus on the Family).

Chapter 25

1. *Strong's Greek/Hebrew Dictionary* (Biblesoft & International Bible Translators, 1994).

Chapter 32

1. *Brown, Driver, & Briggs Hebrew Lexicon* (Ontario: Online Bible, 1993).

Chapter 34

1. Rela M. Geffen et al., *Celebration and Renewal: Rights of Passage in Judaism* (Philadelphia and Jerusalem: The Jewish Publication Society, 1993), 62-63.

2. Grace Ketterman, M.D., *Rebellion, Can It Be Prevented?: Parents and Teenagers* (Wheaton: Victor Books, 1984), 483.

Chapter 35

1. Dr. James Dobson, 7, April 2000. www.family.org

2. Ibid

3. Ibid

Chapter 40

1. *Nelson's Illustrated Bible Dictionary.* (Nashville: Thomas Nelson, 1986).

Chapter 46

1. 7, April, 2000 available from http://www.family.org.

   For more information regarding *Exodus International,* call 206-784-7799 (US only call toll-free 888-264-0877), or write
   Exodus International
   P.O. Box 77652
   Seattle, WA 98177.

Chapter 47

1. Eric Schlosser, "The Business of Pornography," *U.S. News & World Report,* 10 February 1997.

2. Ibid.

3. Dr. Gene Able, 7, April 2000; available from http://www.family.org/pastor/resources/sos/a0006643.html.

4. W. Marshall, "Report on the Use of Pornography by Sexual Offenders," *Report to the Federal Department of Justice* (Ottawa: 1983).

5. 7, April 2000; available from http://www.family.org/pastor/resources/sos/a0006643.html.

Chapter 49

1. Kathleen Winkler with Melissa Brunette, "A Diet to Die For," *Single-Parent Family,* 1998, 7, April 2000; available from http://www.family.org/pplace/youandteens/a006050.html.

2. Ibid.

3. Ibid.

4. "An Eating Disorder Can Eat You Alive," part 1 of 3, *Brio Magazine,* November 1998. 7, April 2000; available from http://www.family.org/pplace/girls/briomag/features/a0003301.html.

5. Winkler, "A Diet to Die For."